DOUGLAS MAYO

Douglas first took to the amateur stage in a production of *The White Horse Inn* for the Parramatta New Theatre Company in Sydney, Australia. It wasn't long before he realised that he much preferred working behind-the-scenes in marketing and publicity, and eventually in producing musicals.

For the next ten years, he produced shows, established theatre groups and had a finger in all aspects of production, including the occasional onstage cameo when a silent walk-on part beckoned.

At age 22, he commissioned and professionally staged the full-length concert musical version of Mike Batt's *The Hunting Of The Snark* and launched the first show by Australian comedy duo *The Umbilical Brothers*. He toured a series of one man shows and helped to develop several new musicals.

In 1994/5 he was a co-producer of one of the world's first amateur productions of *Les Miserables* which ran for 42 performances with over 40,000 people attending the show.

Based in London, Douglas is now Editor of *Amateur Stage Magazine* where he continues to stimulate interest in amateur theatre and encourages development of modern theatre practice.

www.amateurstagemagazine.co.uk

PACKED TO THE RAFTERS

2012 Edition

How to publicise your show on a budget.

A guide for school, amateur and fringe theatre.

Douglas Mayo

Edited by Phil Matthews

SILVERMOON PUBLISHING
London
www.silvermoonpublishing.co.uk

PACKED TO THE RAFTERS

First published in Great Britain in October 2012
by Silvermoon Publishing
3rd Floor, 207 Regent Street, London, W1B 3HH

Cover photograph by Peter Cook.
Copyright Royal Shakespeare Company.

Author photograph by www.actorheadshots.co.uk
Typeset by Amateur Stage Magazine & Martin Louw.

Edited by Phil Matthews.

A CIP catalogue record for this book is available
from the British Library.

ISBN 978 1 84094 877 6

For Judy & Jim.
Thank you for your continued support.

Contents

Acknowledgements

You can read a lot of books, but a lot of the learning comes from the doing. There have been many successes and failures along the way, but most of the outcomes arose from the efforts applied in PR and marketing. I learned the hard way, that you disregard its importance at your peril.

I need to thank Neil who was there on day one. I still have the scrap of paper with the scribbling's of two lunatics to prove it. He encouraged me to get out there and act on my dreams.

To the many people who helped me to promote shows and helped me learn the "How To" by doing it for real. Thank you.

Thank you to Paul, who has been my friend and partner in helping restore the fortunes of Amateur Stage since that fateful day when we decided to take it on.

Thanks to Julian Cound, Pippa Roome and Stephen Beeny for their assistance with the Case Studies for this book.

Special thanks to Phil Matthews who inspired me to write it all down and then whipped it into shape.

INTRODUCTION

It really doesn't matter how good your show is, without an audience, it's all for nothing.

Strong words perhaps for those out there doing this for the artistic love of it. But our efforts would be for nought if we performed a brilliant show to an empty theatre.

Anyone who has ever performed to an auditorium where the cast outnumbers the audience will tell you that.

It needn't be that way however. No matter how big (or small) your theatre is, and no matter what show you are presenting, it is possible to find an audience to appreciate it. In some cases they'll come running, in others it might be the sales job of the century, but the key to either result is basic organisation and planning, thinking through all of your options and applying a plan to attract an audience.

I've tried to keep the contents of this book as concise as possible. I would urge the reader to read the book in its entirety first. Try to avoid skipping ahead to specific chapters if you can. Planning a modern PR campaign means looking at an integrated whole, not ad-hoc projects. I hope that in doing so you might get new insight into a side of PR that you've often taken for granted.

During the course of this book, I will impart all of the valuable information I learnt promoting successful shows and the lessons learned from those not so successful, so that you might avoid it.

There will, of course, be times when outside forces threaten to knock your plan off track. I've had shows suffer at the hands of televised wars and celebrity health scares. The sign of a good PR team is your ability to adapt. Quick thinking and the capacity to see the possibilities in an idea, can keep show publicity ticking along.

The days of 'set it and forget it' PR are now gone however. Promoting your show will take constant effort. Don't be afraid to look at your efforts everyday to see what else you could do based on current events. I spoke to two amateur groups here in the UK that I admire greatly. Darlington Operatic Society and SEDOS are two very different organisations, but both work brilliantly (and in varied ways) to ensure that their shows sell. Over my years as Editor of Amateur Stage I have seen them implement some of the most creative marketing campaigns. They understand their audiences, the importance of social media and, most importantly, getting their casts involved in the PR effort. Their achievements are worth looking at if you want an idea of just how to pull off a successful PR campaign.

I trust that you will find the contents of this guide informative, inspiring and thought-provoking. I'm looking forward to seeing the results of some of the campaigns resulting from Packed to the Rafters as they come across my desk (that's a broad hint that I want to be on your media list by the way!).

Finally, whether your group is large or small, a drama group or one dedicated to staging musicals, the principals found in this book can be applied to everyone. Be creative and use your resources in the best way you can. Don't be afraid though to try new things, in most cases it won't cost you money to try a different approach, so what have you got to lose? In my experience, fear of change exists with the group themselves, the outside world really doesn't even think about it. Try thinking outside your comfort zone!

Implement your plan correctly and you will fast become one of the most valued assets of your theatre company.

Douglas Mayo
London, 2012
editor@asmagazine.co.uk

1. ONE PR OR A CACOPHONY OF PRS?

Can one person handle the workload?

Being the PR person for a theatre group can often be a thankless task. You are often the unsung hero of the piece. If you do your job well, your efforts will often go unnoticed as focus falls on the quality of the show itself.

It's not surprising therefore, in this modern day and age, that many groups have a revolving door operating when it comes to their PR person. People think that it is a lot of work and they would be right.

It is possible for one person to do the job of the theatre PR, but I would suggest that your group will be better served with a small team of people each taking on the responsibility for a different area of the publicity process (media, flyers, sponsorship, cast liaison), with one person in charge of delegation and oversight.

This split responsibility will also mean less pressure on your team and hopefully give them some longevity, not to mention making the process a bit more sociable.

It is always possible that a member of your team will not get on with certain media contacts. The science of personality means that not everyone clicks. It is therefore important to identify any problems quickly and if necessary get another member of your team dealing with the media contact in question. Don't stress – just get someone else who does 'click' with the contact to keep the process rolling.

Try not to replace the entire team in one go. Keeping some of the team on-board when new members join will help maintain continuity. New members can be bought up-to-speed by members who are familiar with how your system operates.

THE BASICS
A tight team will make sure that every aspect of the PR process is covered and that your group gives the outward appearance of being professional in the way that they handle the press.

One important thing to consider is that at least two of your team per production should not be on stage. Part of the PR process requires face-to-face time front-of-house during shows looking after the press and special guests. As PR representative, the last thing you want to be doing is worrying about how the press are being treated when you are backstage waiting in the wings for your entrance. I realise in smaller groups this may be a luxury, but do the best that you can. One of the strengths of amateur and fringe groups is their ability to improvise when it comes to resource management.

Sure, this task can be delegated to a non-PR team member of the company, but the impact of that personal contact and the building of the relationship that this face-to-face time engenders, can't be duplicated to the same effect by anyone not on the team. The meet-and-greet function of the job will enable you to get valuable information from the media, which will help you in your future endeavours. Make a point of taking notes after the start of each show, including anyone met by the PR representatives, along with any pertinent comments to add to your database.

You'd be surprised what can be learned on these occasions. Many years ago, I had one regional editor let slip that if we had a decent full colour 'costumed publicity photo' available the week after we began rehearsals, he could have given us a full colour image on the cover of his newspaper. A missed opportunity when you consider it had 90% of our audience within its reach. We just didn't realise that by submitting the self same photo six weeks later we had missed the boat. A bit of inconvenience on our part gave us a huge lift in sales for each of our subsequent shows.

Remember your job is to work with the press and media (radio, TV and internet) to get results. Sometimes this means altering the way you work to accommodate what they need.

Once you have devised a list of the jobs and responsibilities that need to be met, it can be easily divided amongst members of the team. Regular 'update' meetings can keep control of the PR campaign and look at modifications that need to be undertaken if deemed necessary.

You will be surprised at how easily tasks can be undertaken and performed once your team settles into a routine.

You must consider the future though at all points during the process. Make notes and keep constantly updated databases with relevant information relating to each contact. If one of your team drops out, you need to be able to bring someone else up to speed quickly.

Also, the more copious your notes are, the easier you will find planning the campaign for your next production.

Chapter 1 - Thoughts & actions

• Build a team, share the responsibilities and workload.

• Have some of your team offstage to deal with PR efforts during the run.

• Keep an up-to-date database of press contacts for future reference.

• A good PR team must serve the press, and not expect the press to serve them.

2. THE RIGHTS CONTRACT

It's all about billing.

Okay, so your group has decided on a show and secured the performance rights. The minute the rights contract is signed, it is important that your PR team receive a copy of the relevant billing and marketing information relating to the show.

The rights contract will usually specify all of the information you are contractually obliged to mention when promoting your show. Make sure you get this information immediately and make notes relating to everything that is required of you. Contracts can be revoked if you get this wrong, so take the time to understand what you are required to do.

Whilst sometimes you will sit there wondering why you have to list the original Broadway producer or director. The fact remains, that if the contract requires it, then you have to do it. If something isn't clear, then call the rights holder: they don't bite and they would much rather help you get it right than have to scold you for getting it wrong.

Sometimes contracts will specify that the names of composers or associated parties need to be shown in specified ratios to other names. For example, the name of the composers must be no less than 10% of the size of the show title on your handbill and/or posters. In most cases this doesn't need to be to the exact millimetre. You can certainly judge the intention when designing your material. Keep a copy of the rights contract handy at all times. You'll be surprised how many times you'll be referring to it.

Last, but not least, double check the spelling of all of the details you are required to include when preparing your material. You'd be surprised how many times groups get it wrong. Form a checklist that includes dates, performance times, venue, contact numbers for bookings, website, etc. amongst other items.

Chapter 2 - Thoughts and actions

• Know your contractual billing requirements from day one.

• Keep a copy on-hand at all times.

• Ensure that you spell the names of creatives correctly (Composer, playwright, director, etc.)

3. RESEARCH – PART ONE

*So just how much do your PR team know
about your show?*

Your group has selected a show and the rights have been secured. You have all the information you need for the billing and contractual obligations relating to it.

The next question becomes just how much does your PR team know about the show you are staging? How much do you know about what your creative team is planning?

This is where you can really come into your own as a publicity team. You are now tasked with finding out as much as you can. Some of the information you will need includes:-

• A brief outline of the plot;

• A brief history of the show itself. When it opened, awards won, famous previous cast members and any trivia about the show will come in handy;

• Any previous publicity material or reviews for the show you can find. Quotes from this can be used in your pre-publicity material;

• Does the show have a website or fan site on Facebook or Twitter? Don't forget that there are always die-hard fans who will travel to see a show they love;

• Information about your creative team – who are they? What have they done before?

• Start compiling factoids about your show – for example, the fact that you'll be using 600 costumes during the run, or that you are using specially imported gore for those special make-up effects. Press love factoids like these, so do some legwork and find them out.

By the end of this process you should have a bundle of information that can be included in your press materials. This can be especially useful if you are doing a new show that isn't well known. Back history can make most shows sound great. You need to convince your audience that it's worth seeing, and the show's history is the first step in the process.

I'm assuming that as a PR team you will also be helping to publicise auditions. Information gathered during this process should be used to compile the audition brief for your show. Make the production sound exciting and your creative team sound incredible. This will be 'the' show to be in.

Once you have all the information, take the time to edit it down into a few brief pages. Your PR team should be well-informed and know this information backwards before embarking on any press activity. You need to have information in your head ready to go – no hesitations or uncertainty.

In short – KNOW YOUR SHOW!

Chapter 3 - Thoughts and actions

• Do thorough research on the show you are staging.

• Compile a show profile including historic information and factoids that can be used for press purposes.

4. RESEARCH – PART TWO

*Now you have the basics, you need to
know so much more.*

You've held auditions and you now have a cast. That's great, but how much do you know about them?

It's Day One of rehearsals (or earlier if possible) and the first thing the PR team will do is distribute a questionnaire to all cast asking some basic questions including:-

• Personal details (within reason);
• Where do they work? Do they have an unusual occupation?
• Reasons why they wanted to do the show?
• What magazines do they read?
• What are their local papers?
• Interesting facts about themselves – amazing feats, world records, interesting hobbies – anything they care to divulge.

Don't go crazy, but you can see where I am going with this. You may uncover the fact that your leading man is a former Olympic athlete, you may even discover that the editor of your local paper was best man at his wedding. Every contact and bit of information is potentially helpful when trying to pitch to the media. The more angles you have, the more likely you are to get a story published.

Take the information and compile it. You may find some cast members live outside your area giving you potential access to other local media. Get the bigger picture before you start to outline your PR campaign. Make best use of your resources.

Take the time to talk to every cast member. Some will be shy, but you'll find others are natural 'talkers' who will make for great interview subjects. If a radio interview is available, you have an ideal candidate ready to go. Highlight natural strengths and file them away ready for use as the media demands.

This may sound harsh, but I've even seen a campaign run to attract more men using some of the newer more 'photogenic' women from the cast. Bold, indeed. Especially in the politically correct world we now live in.

Look at your resources and use them appropriately to publicise your show and build your brand. Don't follow ideas blindly, ultimately you are the arbiter of what best suits your group and how you want the public to perceive you.

Chapter 4 - Thoughts and actions

- Know your cast by collecting profile information on them.

- Find 'talking heads' who you can use as natural interview subjects.

5. RESEARCH PART THREE

So who are you going to tell?

Take the time to sit down and develop the ultimate hit list for your PR campaign. Check out all of your local papers, radio stations, local and national magazines, websites, trade organisations, schools, universities, and anyone else who might be able to help you spread the word.

Take the time to investigate smaller media as well. Church bulletins, school newsletters, social group newsletters and smaller community magazines are worth your time. Bigger media outlets may be more prestigious, but it is highly possible that your audience is likely to be from the local community and therefore better reached by community media.

Now really look at the list you have compiled. Have you really exploited it? For instance, in your local paper there may be a main news desk, an arts reporter, listings section, and possibly a business section, amongst others. Sending one press release to the newspaper won't cut it. You need to approach each of these sections with information specifically prepared for them. For instance, the news-desk should receive a general release with broad information. The arts reporter should receive a release but also information about attending to review the show. The listings section should receive information structured to fit the way the publication lists shows and the business editor, a release outlining how a company has recently sponsored your group or show.

Don't just assume that the one release you send will get to everyone who needs to see it. Also, don't assume that the press have time to delve through mountains of information for what they need. Most modern media outlets now are working with fewer staff, so they rely on you as PR to edit the material down to its most relevant form. In fact, it has been known for some papers to reprint a release, word-for-word, if it is well written.

Whilst I'm not criticising lazy media, I'm just saying that with some careful forethought, you might just end up with four mentions in your local paper rather than just one.

Once you have listed all of the potential targets for your media blitz, make a point of finding out their deadlines. Don't forget that monthly magazines work to different deadlines than daily newspapers. You may find your information is required eight weeks before the show opens for one publication and two weeks before for another. It is your job as PR to ensure that information is received in a manner that is timely to the publication you are targeting. (See Chapter 11 on writing your media release)

DEADLINES ARE IMPORTANT! MISS THEM AT YOUR PERIL.

I know this means more work, but the pay-off can be sizeable and your media contacts will appreciate you all the more for being pro-active in finding out what they require.

Chapter 5 - Thoughts and actions

- Develop a media hit list.

- Deadlines are not to be missed.

- Media is not a hit and miss affair – take the time to send out releases and information to everyone.

- Find out what each media outlet needs – don't just send what you think is correct.

6. BUDGET

*Possibly the most important word in
any PR Campaign.*

Before commencing on any PR activities, it is important to liaise with your committee to agree a PR Budget. In today's climate it would be suicidal to think that a PR budget was not necessary, and that a show could be promoted for free.

Whilst we will discuss many aspects of free PR in this book, you will need to tightly budget the myriad of small costs associated with promoting your show. Even the cost of the humble postage stamp must be taken into account along with items such as paper, telephone calls and mailing list software, amongst other things.

You also need guidance as to whether you will be responsible for flyers, posters, newspaper or radio advertising, which could cost considerably more.

I once saw an interview with the successful West End producer Cameron Mackintosh, who claimed that 33% of his pre-production budget for any show was allocated to PR and marketing. Now, even though we don't anticipate that our shows will run for more than a few weeks let alone a few years, the importance of the marketing budget and how it is allocated must be looked at. It is important to evaluate the "professionalism" of having posters and flyers produced by a printing company rather than a member of the group's inkjet printer (or much worse) hand-written posters and flyers.

When approaching your show budget, it's a great idea to employ a technique that my mother used to apply to sample bags at the local horticultural show. Her philosophy went something along the lines of 'pick up everything you can that costs nothing, before spending a penny on anything else'. Sage words in my opinion. The translation – work out everything you can do as a PR team before you spend any money. It is amazing just how much publicity can be had without spending a dime. Don't rush into spending money, make your list as comprehensive as possible before taking this next step.

Then and only then, draw up a list of things that are likely to cost money in promoting your show. Always assume that you will have to pay for everything that remains. Remember though, everything is negotiable. Budgeting for a worst-case scenario can only leave you better off if various items on your list are donated or fall under a sponsorship arrangement. Make sure you budget honestly, don't just assume that individuals in your PR group will bear the costs of the numerous phone calls, couriers or petrol involved in promoting your show. There's no faster way of losing your PR helpers if it costs them to help. Some won't mind, of course, but never presume.

Chapter 6 - Thoughts and actions

- Ascertain all your free forms of media coverage.

- Be honest when you budget PR expenses and costs.
  You can always come in under budget.

- Don't assume that members of your team will be happy
  paying for PR costs no matter how small.

- When purchasing or negotiating PR budget items,
  don't be afraid to employ the 'art of negotiation'.

7. TRACKING YOUR CAMPAIGN

You need to know what is working for you.

One of the most overlooked aspects of any PR campaign is tracking. I'm not talking about what articles, interviews or listings get published, but rather how your PR efforts impact on that most important indicator of all 'The Box Office'.

As the PR team, you need to be copied in on a box office report at least once a week, if not daily, outlining sales for each performance in the run.

You need to be able to gauge on a day-to-day basis how many tickets are sold and to which performances they relate, so that you can accurately assess your PR efforts. For instance, do you see an immediate spike when you run a print or radio advertisement? Is your early bird group bookers offer working? Did the full page interview in your local paper attract any ticket sales? If so, how long before you saw that interview result in sales for future reference.

It is possible that a £1000 investment in radio advertising will yield £5000 in sales. You must be in a position to argue your case for spending and just like any company in the real world, you need sales data to support your case.

Most importantly, if tracking indicates that something works, it is worthwhile trying it again. Does repeat use of a PR method diminish with further use or does it simply build momentum (hopefully the latter) by giving patrons greater exposure to your shows?

Imagine the knowledge base you can build up after tracking two or three shows? One group recently informed me that they were selling 30% more tickets online and 25% more overall at the same time than for a previous show. How did they know? Tracking!

I know that many groups will have the obstinate person who clings to information and doesn't want to give it to anyone else, but on this one you must insist they yield the information to the PR team. You can't do your job properly without it.

In the case of tracking, there is no such thing as too much information. Apart from immediate sales data and its reaction to PR efforts, you could also look at payment methods, online versus traditional booking methods, group booking data, and any age or other demographic data that is collected.

Chapter 7 - Thoughts and actions

- Tracking of your PR efforts is a must.

- Ensure you get the information you need daily if possible.

- Repeat successful efforts in the hope of increasing returns.

- Examine your statistics and compare against future shows.

- Start noting what works in PR for you and what doesn't to refine your activities.

8. CONTACT

*What good is a PR team if no one can
get in touch with you?*

Before you start sending out information about your show,
it is important that you work out a contact structure so that
any and all enquiries are dealt with quickly and efficiently.

A lot of goodwill and potential coverage is lost when groups
are either unable to be contacted or are slow to respond.
Contrary to popular belief, most media outlets work fast
and with limited manpower. With ever-tighter deadlines,
your story is likely to be picked up and published if the
media outlet involved can reach you quickly.

Ideally, the PR team has to be able to respond to an email
or phone message inside of 2-5 hours, often sooner. A few
days or even a week later will often mean that valuable
media coverage is lost. I know from experience that editors
often favour groups that they know can help them quickly
and efficiently. If a last minute space opens up in a magazine
or newspaper, as a journalist, you will always head towards
a reliable source first.

PR CONTACT BASICS

Email
Do you have a dedicated PR email address? It's a must have
item when it comes to handling PR requests for a show.
Usually your webmaster can help you set up a publicity@
email address, but if you have several people spreading

the load of handling PR, it is worth considering setting up a Hotmail or Google account that can be checked by your team on a rotating basis as each has spare time. With the latter option, you and your team can log-in wherever they are and instantly deal with any requests or questions. Personally, I'd try to avoid the Hotmail or G-Mail route if possible. Many domain hosts will also offer an email option for remote collection of email and this should be used if available. publicity@downtownplayers.co.uk will always have a more professional feel than downtownplayers@ hotmail.com.

This email address should be visible on your website and on all of the material you are sending out about the show.

I cannot stress enough though - You must be contactable all or most of the time.

Too many groups get publicity contacts routed through the main group email, and from experience, this means a journalist or editor will either never get a response, or the response will invariably be too late as the main society email isn't checked often enough.

Phone
If you have someone who can take calls at work or someone who works from home who can accept PR calls, that's all well and good, but most groups don't have this luxury.

Yes, you can get calls recorded on an answering machine at home or even on your own mobile, but a simpler and more professional solution is to purchase a cheap 'pay as you go' mobile. This phone can then be passed around as necessary, yet the number remains constant. Answering machine messages can be personalised and the mobility of the phone allows the PR team the opportunity for quick responses. A £10 investment in a cheap phone can help you get hundreds of pounds of publicity just by being contactable. Don't forget that whilst many of you are doing shows for fun and enjoyment, for the media you are contacting, it is a job. Deadlines and time are everything.

A (possibly cheaper) alternative to mobile phones is a "non-geographic" phone number (in the UK 0844, 0845, 0870, etc). Many of these are cheap to buy (some even earn you revenue) and most can have a 'switchboard function' applied to them that you can alter via a website. You can set up a structure that says "press 1 for tickets, press 2 for publicity ..." (or whatever you want). The number that rings when someone presses a button, can be altered at will whenever that officer is unavailable and most will have an option for a alternative number if the primary number goes unanswered.

We will talk in other chapters about quick response tools, but for now ensuring the media can reach you is paramount. In an age of smart phones, being non-contactable is no longer an excuse.

Face-to-face
Throughout the publicity process your PR team will be in face-to-face situations with press and other useful contacts.

It is of the highest importance on each of these occasions that you present yourselves professionally and efficiently.

Some basics:-

• Don't be late, always be early.

• Be prepared and informed. Know the name of the person you are meeting and some salient facts about them. Always greet them by name.

• Smile! It may sound silly, but you are more likely to appear positive and get a positive result when you smile.

• Dress smartly and present yourself well. If at all possible, having a business card is a good idea when meeting a media person or any potential business contact.

The face-to-face extends from day one of your PR odyssey through to performances. Make sure you set up a Press/VIP desk so that important contacts don't have to queue. Welcome them to your show personally.

Face-to-face greeting enables you to establish a relationship with your contacts that goes beyond an email or voice on the telephone. Take advantage and build that relationship, and it can be mutually beneficial.

Chapter 8 - Thoughts and actions

- Make sure the media can contact you immediately.

- Respond quickly to requests.

- At the very least, have phone and email contact points.

- Establish a personal relationship with media contacts wherever possible.

- Be prompt, prepared and informed.

9. BRANDING

*"A particular identity or image regarded
as an asset" - Oxford Dictionary*

Branding is not just about getting your target audience to choose your show over that of your competition, it is also about getting your audience to identify you as their first port of call when seeking entertainment.

Branding gets right to the core of your company's values.

Whilst that is perhaps a bit high-handed and idealistic for the amateur and fringe theatre marketplace, it is important to consider the "amateur theatre" or "fringe theatre" brand as well as your own company brand. There is no doubt that we can all be tarred with a brush based on a dodgy show or poor theatre experience. As a sector, we need to be aware of the culture of amateur theatre and present ourselves professionally when promoting the brand. Whether we like it or not, if a neighbouring group works hard to make their customer experience exceptional, any neighbouring group receives at least part of any resulting goodwill. Likewise, treating audiences poorly will impact on other groups in your area. It is important that every theatre company works hard to make every audience experience the best it can be. Not all groups have the same resources, but we can treat our audiences with care and respect and be the best that we can be.

How a brand can add value.
Past experience often indicates that customers expect

to pay more for a branded product than for unbranded products. Would you expect to pay the same for a can of a supermarket's own lemonade as you would for a brand you recognise?

You can apply your brand to a whole range of your other products or services. This will allow consumers to associate each product in your range with a consistent set of values which they know.

Also, if you want to extend your product range, consumers' perception of the new offering will be enhanced by your existing brand. By consistently applying your brand attributes, your business can move into new market sectors without changing your core brand identity.

As a PR team you need to consider how you intend to convey your brand to the public.

The objectives that a good brand will achieve include:-

- Delivers your message clearly;
- Confirms your credibility;
- Connects to your audiences emotionally;
- Motivates your audiences to buy;
- Cements user loyalty.

To succeed in branding, you must understand the needs and wants of your customers and prospects. You do this by integrating your brand strategies through your company at every point of public contact.

Your brand resides within the hearts and minds of your audiences, clients and prospects. It is the sum total of their experiences and perceptions, some of which you can influence, and some that you cannot.

A strong brand is invaluable as the battle for customers intensified day-by-day. It's important to spend time investing in researching, defining and building your brand. After all, your brand is the source of a promise to your consumer. It's a foundation piece in your marketing communication and one you do not want to be without.

When you contract any well-known show, you are buying into their brand. Audiences often think fondly about a production of say *Les Miserables*. As a PR team your challenge is to harness that brand and add it to your own successfully.

Harnessing the brand can be as simple as using the same logo as the professional production if it is available. Why would any group want to re-design a logo for a show like *Les Miserables*? The original Producer has invested millions world-wide making it a known symbol with brand value.

Treat your brand carefully, it's hard to build and very easy to damage through neglect or lack of care. Ensure wherever possible that your cast and FOH staff wear any branded clothing or merchandising to re-enforce your professional approach.

Take time to ensure that your logo appears in a constant format throughout your marketing materials, that you stick to assigned colours in logo printing, that materials constantly mention your group name in the same format and that web addresses and other information is in a constant format. You will soon get to a point where your identity is immediately recognisable by your audience and that recognition is invaluable.

Chapter 9 - Thoughts and actions

• Consider the branding of amateur theatre as a whole, not just that of your company.

• Branding can add value to your company.

• Define your brand carefully.

• Discuss how you intend to convey your brand message to the public.

• If possible use the established brand image created by professional productions. Creating your own look for a show may not necessarily be to your benefit.

• Ensure consistency in branding.

10. IMITATE YOUR RIVALS

Why re-invent the wheel?

Imitation may be the sincerest form of flattery, but it can also be a valuable marketing tool.

Keep a constant eye out to see what your rivals do, how professional shows present themselves and even how normal businesses promote themselves. If you see something that appears to work, or that you feel could be adapted to your projects, then look at how you might appropriate it for your own uses.

Why waste time and money trying out a marketing or PR concept if someone else has proven it doesn't work. Similarly, you might see something that has been tried before and see where that campaign fell short or missed a trick. Your adaptation of their campaign might prove profitable.

Chapter 10 - Thoughts and actions

- It's not just a case of imitating your rival theatre group, look at how other companies outside of theatre present themselves.

11. THE PRESS RELEASE

The one document you can't do without.

The "Press Release" in many cases will be your primary communication mechanism with most of the press you are approaching to help publicise your show.

It is important that you have spent time on it, and have it ready to go, before you contact anyone.

So, what is a Press Release?
A Press Release is a document, which contains an overview of your group, your show and the performance details. It should clearly give the media a point of contact for your theatre company to arrange further interviews, articles, or reviews, should they have further questions.

The Press Release is your pitching document. It is your way of suggesting to any editor or media outlet that your event is worthy of their attention and will be of huge interest to their readers.

Most people will tell you that they know how to write a Press Release. In my tenure as a magazine editor, I can assure you that they do not. On a near daily basis I am inundated with hastily scrawled paragraphs, incoherent information which is cut and pasted into emails from other sources, emails proclaiming a new show season but where vital information like dates and venues are omitted, just to name a few.

IMPORTANT TIP
Take the time to get your Press Release right. Nothing will make you look more stupid than having to send multiple revisions of the same document.

A few basics to consider when preparing your release:-

1. *Length* - A news release should be typed and be no longer than two pages if humanly possible.

2. *Date the release* - It helps an editor to know what to do with a release when they can date it. Just imagine how much information flows into a newspaper or magazine office on a daily basis. If your release is dated, it helps any busy editor place it for consideration.

3. *Create a headline* - Once again, editors are busy people, so they need a quick headline that tells them what they are looking at. Your headline doesn't need to be clever, just informative. "ESSEX YOUTH THEATRE STAGE LES MISERABLES" is an example of a short punchy heading that conveys the basis of the release.

4. *The Rule of Diminishing Importance* - Start your release with the most important information going onwards, to the least important information. Your opening paragraph should briefly summarise the important questions of Who? What? Where? When? Don't be vain – the name of your theatre group may not be the most important piece of information. In some cases, people will come to your show because of the show itself. People who will come to see the show because it's your theatre group is already loyal to you and is an easy market. You need to look after them, not sell to them.

5. *Keep it brief* - Don't ramble. Imagine you are writing the article yourself. Write cleanly and without personal comments or asides. Adding personal reminiscences or comments is unprofessional.

6. *Identify yourself!* - Make sure that the release clearly outlines who you are (possibly through the use of your company logo).

7. *Point of Contact* - I've spoken elsewhere in the book about the importance of a primary contact for press. I know that most amateurs have day jobs but expecting a media editor to call you out-of-hours just won't happen. You need to be available when they are and work within their deadlines. Make sure your release has detailed contact information including name, phone number, email address and website.

8. *Check spelling and punctuation, grammar and accuracy* - Nothing infuriates editors more than misspelt or incorrect information, with poor punctuation.

9. *Don't make them sound too parochial* - A Press Release is a professional calling card for your group. Make it sound professional and not too chummy.

GETTING THE MOST OUT OF YOUR RELEASES.

Thinking that just one Press Release will suffice for any given show is archaic. As PR for your group, it is important that you not only utilise existing opportunities but create more.

It is possible to create a range of releases for any given show that enable your group to get continual coverage from the press. Some examples of Press Release subjects include:-

1. **Rights acquisition** – your group is the first to be given rights to a major new show or a production just released for amateurs. Perhaps you have been granted the regional premiere.

2. **Audition notices** – details of the forthcoming auditions for your show and any challenges that may present.

3. **Announce the show** – tell the press when tickets go on sale for your season along with the season details.

4. **Casting announcements** - If your cast is regionally diverse, take the time to target newspapers outside your normal hit list. Chances are if a cast member will travel to you to perform, their supporters or people they know will follow to support them. It is not unheard of at this stage for groups to prepare upwards of twenty different releases for different media outlets focusing on different cast members.

5. **Calamitous releases** - Has your hall flooded? Has your leading man broken a leg? Turn it into a positive event by writing a release about it and make it news. A bit of "media drama" about your drama can often help keep your show in the public's minds and that's not a bad thing.

6. **Box office smashes** - If your show is selling better than you ever expected and shows are selling out, issue a release to that effect. There's nothing better for your on-going attempts at PR than if your current show sells out. People will have to be quick next time to get a ticket.

7. *The Celebrity Release* – Did the author of the play or musical, or a local celebrity pay your group a visit? Make sure you have a photographer on hand and get a release written highlighting the visit. Nothing helps you get more coverage than the involvement of a celebrity or notable person.

8. *After the event* - Sometimes a harder sell, but nevertheless a release outlining the success of a given show after the event can get you some coverage especially in a slow news week. Sometimes editors will thank you for helping to fill holes in their publications. The trick is finding the right balance between being helpful and being a hindrance.

DIFFERENT STORIES FOR DIFFERENT PUBLICATIONS

There is nothing worse than every publication running the same story. Whilst general news stories about your show are fine, don't try to pitch specific angle stories to more than one media source in the same medium. If you feel there might be a conflict where the same story might run in competing magazines, always ask the editor if they have any objection. If you promise an exclusive (ie, a particular story negotiated with one publication only), be prepared to stick to your agreement. Exclusivity helps sell papers and if your supposed exclusive isn't exclusive – well let's just say your next PR campaign may be dead before you start as editors have long memories.

A Sample Release

THE WANDERING MINSTRELS PRESENT HAIRSPRAY THE MUSICAL

Following their sell-out success with *Bye Bye Birdie*, The Wandering Minstrels head back to the 60's to an era of huge hair with the smash hit musical *Hairspray*, which will be performed at the Google Theatre, Richmond, from the 13th – 19th September 2012.

This production of *Hairspray* will be the largest amateur production ever staged and will utilise the West End sets and costumes. Direction will be provided by original West End cast member Tom Dickenson, who having performed with the group in his youth is returning to help pass on some of his professional experience.

Harry Hodgpodge (who recently won rave reviews for his portrayal of Conrad Birdie in the company's production of *Bye Bye Birdie*) will take on the larger-than-life role of Edna Turnblatt, alongside Tina Turley as Tracey, her dance-addicted daughter. Further casting to be announced.

HAIRSPRAY - based on the John Waters film of the same name, has enjoyed award-winning seasons both on Broadway and in London's West End, before embarking on sell-out national tours delighting millions.

Show composers, Marc Shaiman and Scott Witman, between them have had considerable success as the composers of award-winning songs like *Wind Beneath My Wings*, the musical *Catch Me If You Can*, the TV series *Smash* and the soon to open West End musical *Charlie and the Chocolate Factory.*

The Wandering Minstrels are proud to announce that a percentage of their ticket sales for their season of *Hairspray* will be donated to UK Cancer Research, whose work for children with cancer is groundbreaking.

Hairspray is being presented by arrangement with Josef Weinberger in association with Music Theatre International.

For more information please visit
www.thewanderingminstrels.co.uk

LISTINGS INFORMATION
HAIRSPRAY THE MUSICAL

Written by Scott Witman and Marc Shaiman
Book by Thomas Meehan
Directed by Tom Dickenson
Opening Night : Thursday 13 September 2012
Google Theatre, High Street, Richmond, SW22 5GT
Box Office 0845 666 7777
For further media enquiries please contact
Eddie Foghorn
Press Liaison
The Wandering Minstrels
P O Box 75
Richmond SW22 3EQ

Direct: 07731 444 673
E: press@wanderingminstrels.co.uk

Notes for editors.

Hairspray is a musical with music by Marc Shaiman, lyrics by Scott Wittman and Shaiman and a book by Mark O'Donnell and Thomas Meehan, based on the 1988 John Waters film *Hairspray* starring Ricki Lake. The songs include 1960's-style dance music and "downtown" rhythm and blues. In 1962 Baltimore, Maryland, plump teenager Tracy Turnblad's dream is to dance on The Corny Collins Show, a local TV dance program based on the real-life Buddy Deane Show. When Tracy wins a role on the show, she becomes a celebrity overnight. She then launches a campaign to integrate the show. *Hairspray* is a social commentary on the injustices of parts of American society in the 1960's.

The musical's original Broadway production opened on August 15, 2002 and won eight Tony Awards out of thirteen nominations. It ran for over 2,500 performances and closed on 4 January 2009. *Hairspray* has also had national tours, a London West End production, and numerous foreign productions and was adapted as a 2007 musical film. The London production was nominated for a record-setting eleven Laurence Olivier Awards, winning for Best New Musical and in three other categories.

The Wandering Minstrels have been performing locally for the past 65 years. Starting as a small group of 20 performers, they now have over 200 actors who range from 12 to 80 years of age. Each year, the group performs two major musicals, a pantomime, charity concerts and two plays to an audience exceeding 7000 patrons.

In 2010, the company won the coveted Richmond Times award for *Best Community Group*.

In conclusion.

Once you have your basic release written, ensure that you get someone else to review it. Nothing is more valuable than a second set of eyes to check your work. Do the phone numbers work? Are the correct dates shown? Are the names spelt correctly? Are you complying with your rights contract? Your release must be correct the first time it goes out.

If you do send out a release with an error, don't panic. Correct the errors, double-check the document again and re-send to your media list. Ensure that you include the words "Corrected" or "Revised" in the subject heading and explain that an error was made in the message body. Be careful, you only get one chance to correct. There are no third chances!

It pays to include a copy of the text for your release in an email, as well as attaching the text to the email as a word document. This dual method ensures that the recipient can utilise your information in any way they see fit and with a minimum of effort.

Don't just rely on colour or high resolution images for a press release. Keep fonts simple and readable. Don't use fancy fonts, clipart or special effects.

Finally, it's always worth following up your release with a phone call. Don't nag, but a call to introduce yourself and ascertain the press release has arrived never goes astray and can prompt action.

Chapter 11 - Thoughts and actions

- Press releases are an important tool. Take time to get them right.

- Ensure that your releases contain all the relevant information.

- Numerous specialised releases may be required to get you the best coverage.

- Even bad news can be good news when it comes to PR coverage.

- Have someone double-check your releases. Make sure all the information is correct.

12. PHOTOGRAPHY

One picture can change everything.

How many times have you stopped to read an article in a newspaper or magazine because an interesting picture caught your eye?

Great photography is an essential part of good theatre publicity. Get it right and it works wonders. Get it wrong and your press release will be relegated to the rubbish bin.

Think about it this way. You are the publisher of a magazine or newspaper and you get sent two pictures for two competing shows. One is good quality, thoughtfully staged and eye-catching. The other is of poor quality and bland. Which one do you print?

Achieving great quality photos needn't be difficult, but there are a few things you might want to consider:-

• You should have photography sessions scheduled early in the rehearsal process. The more opportunities you have, the more chances you have to make the press.

• Find a local photographer or even a photography student who is keen to help. If you see great photos in your local paper, try to find out who the photographer is. I've seen photographers helping for free on the basis that they can sell copies of their photos to cast members. Think outside the box. One group I know even asked the local newspaper photographer to take extra pictures for them and slipped him a few extra pounds for his trouble. Most local areas have photographic societies who are frequently looking for opportunities to photograph something different – why not form an alliance with them!

• If you feel that your budget means you have to do it yourself, then do the research. You will need a good digital camera for starters. This isn't such a big ask anymore as most domestic digital cameras have enough resolution for the job. Ensure your camera is set on the highest resolution setting. Yes, your memory card won't hold as many pictures, but that's down to the fact that the images are of higher quality, so an investment in a bigger memory card might be in order. If you are technology phobic, go to your local camera store and ask for help. Most will show you how to adjust the setting without charge. You know you are going wrong if you are submitting photos that are less than 300k in file size. A good image could be between 1 megabyte and in some cases over 8 megabytes in size.

• The practice of sending physical photos to newspapers and magazines is now a thing of the past. Digital photography has made physical photos redundant. You will need to deliver photos on a CD or email. Alternately opening an account with a website like www.flickr.com will allow you to upload your photos to the internet allowing people to download the ones they want. Ensure that each photo is labelled in its subject heading and includes any photographic credit. E.g: Marius at the wedding – Les Miserables – Woking Drama – Photo: Good Snapper. That way, photo information is attached to the image and can be easily accessed by the publication even if the original email gets misplaced. If possible, put the same photo (provided you own copyright or can obtain permission) on your theatre website to help with recognition.

• I've lost count of the number of times groups have told me it would take a week or two to send a picture as the committee needed to approve photos. Make sure that your publicity committee has pre-approved photos available all the time. Work out which photos warrant publication in advance. Keep the media waiting at your peril.

• Keep a track of which photos you are sending to whom. Try to have a number of alternate shots available so you don't end up with two competing publications publishing the same picture.

• Think about how creative use of photography can help you get more PR. We talked about individual press releases in Chapter 11. If you are doing a press release based around a specific cast member, make sure you have suitable imagery to go with it.

• Make the images dramatic. Stage the shot well. If in doubt, spend some time looking through books of theatre photography, or see what types of photographs are being published by local press or national papers. You'll soon see the one thing that makes them special – they are well staged! Generally, a close up or cropped image will publish better than a wide shot where detail is lost. If your show is well-known and images from its professional run exist, don't be afraid to use some creative license in duplicating strong, resonant images. Once again, if the image was well-publicised in its professional life, it will have a recognition factor that may work in your favour with the general public.

• Make sure you get lots of good photos at dress rehearsal.

Don't be afraid to ask the lighting designer to bump the lighting up by 10% just to give you better images. Most won't mind if you ask nicely and are purpose driven – they understand photographers need more light. Show publicity matters and it is in everyone's best interests for the photos to look great. Ensure that decent production images are sent to any reviewers who attend your show. All principals should get a close up shot and that there are other photographs showing two characters in a scene together. This will keep editors happy. Don't leave the media waiting, have it in their email inbox by the next morning. You may even get special requests for photos featuring certain cast members. Be prepared and not too precious if someone is singled out for attention. Yes, that group shot is great, but a photo featuring a person of interest to the reviewer may get more space in the publication.

• When taking publicity shots, consider the background. If you are staging *West Side Story*, finding an old fashioned fire escape might just make for a more interesting photograph. Likewise, a photo near a vintage steam train would work for a play like *The Railway Children*. Being creative in your choice of background can make your photo stand out, giving you more chance of getting it published.

• Make sure you properly credit the photographer and label all photographs accordingly. Many professional PR's will actually rename the photo file with all appropriate information. For example: 'London City Players present Oliver! Ronald Gent as Fagin Photo by Rusty Jones Photography.jpg'.

• Don't be tempted to use fancy effects found in some image editing software. Changing your photos using

Photoshop or other editing software can often render your photograph unusable.

Chapter 12 - Thoughts and actions

- A picture is worth a thousand words.

- You can never have enough photographs available for the press.

- Have approved photos ready to go at a moment's notice. The press won't wait for your committee to meet.

- Offer a range of photographs and ensure they are properly credited for media use.

- Make sure your photos are available digitally.

- Stage your shots carefully.

13. FLYERS

The smallest billboard for your show ever invented.

The flyer or handbill may be the smallest of the marketing items you produce, but there's no doubt that it usually has the most impact when it comes to selling tickets. It is a huge surprise therefore to see some of the efforts produced by groups, and in some cases, how little care or attention is given to this vital marketing tool.

When I first started doing amateur shows in the 1980's, we were still working with hand drawn illustrations, Letraset stencils (you really don't know how much of a boon desktop publishing was until you had to use one of these!) and the use of workplace photocopiers with coloured paper (if you were lucky). Heaven help you if you only had access to a ratty old copier!

Today, the flyer gives audiences an immediate impression of what your show is going to be like. If your flyer is poorly designed and thought-out, chances are the patrons impression of the show will be affected, like it or not.

The flyer is important, so take time to get it right. Get a few variations prepared and select the one that works best. Don't be afraid to be pedantic about the look and feel of your flyer. The time and effort put into making it right will pay off in spades.

Make sure that flyers (and posters) are one of the first things you arrange. Check with your printer for quotes and turnaround times. It always amazes me when you talk to printers and hear their stories about clients looking for overnight turnaround because the company forgot to order flyers for a special event. Get your flyers printed properly. Print-outs from a member's laser printer will not suffice.

I receive hundreds of flyers each month for amateur shows across the UK and on the whole groups are embracing the facilities available and producing promotional material that is equal to, and in some cases, better than their professional counterparts.

If you are unsure where to begin, collect a selection of professional West End or tour flyers. Take a look at how the professionals do it. Chances are there are design fundamentals you can use for your own flyers and posters.

Whether you are looking at posters or flyers, decent design is everything! Many rights holders for musicals can now supply you with logo and graphic kits to help you design flyers that look professional, with many looking just like their West End versions did. Whilst creatively you may have a preference for a logo that is designed especially for your show, nothing beats audience recognition of a familiar logo or type style. Imagine trying to redesign the *Les Miserables* or *Cats* logo – you'd be re-inventing the wheel with little or no possible benefit.

If you are doing a lesser-known play, talk to your printer or designer – there are some theatre printers in the UK who still have libraries of images and previous logos specially designed for the production you are staging. If in doubt, ask. You'll be surprised with what's available. Getting a designer to help you won't cost the earth and will give your finished product that extra 'zing'.

Do not assume that you can simply use a logo that you find online. Artwork is copyrighted and belongs to the artist of the producer who commissioned it. If you find a logo you like, do some research and ask for permission to use it. In many cases you will be allowed to use it for free, in some cases a small fee will apply. But get permission you must. Not seeking aproval could land you with a legal case for copyright infringement worth thousands of pounds.

Please be careful. I have heard some groups give the job of designing a poster to Mr. X because he 'wants a go'. Mr. X has no experience with designing a flyer and sometimes that can work out fine but would you trust your business to a novice? Just because theatre is your hobby doesn't mean you should risk presenting poorly to the public. Think about your brand. Take Mr. X and train him up with the PR group to increase his skills before letting his work loose on the public.

When designing your flyer, think about how it will be made available to the public. If it is on show in a dedicated holder, that's great, but many will be placed in brochure racks where only the top third might be visible. Make the front cover of the leaflet as snappy and professional looking as possible. You can put lots of other information inside but try to keep the cover limited to the name of the show, venue and dates. Unless your company is award-winning with a large following (and as a result, your group name sells), even the name of the group can be relegated to the inside in some cases.

Likewise, make sure the paper stock isn't so thin that the flyer will bend over when standing upright. Spending an extra few pounds on thicker paper might just be in order.

There is a tendency recently to print A5 flyers (210mm high x 148mm wide) rather than DL flyers (210mm high x 99mm wide). I must admit to being a DL fan on almost every occasion, especially when you look at the cost of mailing (A5 costs almost double to post). One of the easiest promotional tricks for groups is to ask supporting companies and members to mail out flyers. You'd be surprised that a local business might include your flyer with their invoices or other promotional material to show their support. A DL flyer can easily be inserted without impacting the cost of post.

At the time of writing, it is possible to get full colour DL flyers printed in the UK for anywhere between £30 and £60 for 2000 flyers.

If you think creatively, it's possible to have the cost of your print entirely covered by advertising or sponsorship. Sponsorship is another more complicated issue, but just ask how many local businesses or restaurants might be interested in buying a third of the back of your flyer to advertise?

Budget permitting, your print can even work harder for you with some planning. An A4 gatefold leaflet, – similar to those produced by professional shows can serve multiple purposes for your group. Designed correctly, the inside can be used as an A4 (210mm x 297mm) poster, whilst the outside contains extra information about the show, booking information, sponsor information and even saleable advertising space that could pay for the print in full and possibly generate a profit for your group.

If you are really creative and get on well with groups in your area, or if you are in a situation where you share your venue with other groups, you might consider a joint collaborative effort that lists multiple shows in one brochure with each group sharing the cost. Distribution is shared and each group benefits by the increased coverage.

One group that I worked with were extremely creative with their flyering. They obtained a local map from the council and divided it up into small blocks that could easily be walked within a few hours. They then prepared small plastic shopping bags full of flyers and stuck the map on the outside. Cast were asked to pick an area and then distribute the flyers to every letterbox shown on their map. Once completed, the map section would be crossed off the master map. With each cast member taking a section, pretty soon most of the local area had received a leaflet about the show and thousands of ticket sales resulted. Flyers got the public familiarised with the show they were staging and it kept the cast healthy too!

Finally, the point of a flyer is to get them out and into the hands of the public. Flyers sitting gathering dust in a rehearsal hall are useless and if left too late, will be worthless.

Chapter 13 - Thoughts and actions

• Don't ignore the humble flyer, it remains one of your best marketing tools.

• Plan your flyer distribution carefully and consider how they will be displayed when designing artwork.

• Get your flyers sponsored by approaching a sponsor.

• Look at sharing your flyer costs with another group to get twice the coverage.

• Don't leave flyers in boxes. Get them out and circulating not gathering dust.

14. POSTERS, BANNERS AND BILLBOARDS

Subliminal advertising at its best.

Posters

In years past, many groups were able to sell out their seasons by placing a number of posters in shop windows and on billboards across town. Sadly, those days are gone, and whilst it is still important to produce and distribute posters, the decline of the UK high street has also seen the decline in the effect of public posters.

That's not to say you shouldn't create posters. Quite the contrary.

Posters, particularly those associated with theatre front-of-house displays, are vital to spreading the word about your show, especially if your venue is continually busy and vibrant.

Think about the amount of footfall traffic passing through the venue and it's environs (restaurants, cafes, etc). As a PR group, you need to look at how others use the venue and its surrounds, and display your posters accordingly. If your potential ticket buyers already know the venue, you are halfway there in persuading them to buy a ticket.

Don't go crazy printing posters. Talk to your cast and ask how many they honestly think they will need and where they could place them for you.

Banners

At one time, many groups would simply paint a huge banner and place it on a fence in public sight to help raise awareness of their show. Sadly, many of those opportunities are gone as councils and other organisations halt banner advertising for public safety reasons.

Start your banner campaign by approaching your local council to ask what permission is needed and what opportunities exist for banners. It can be a minefield but one that is worth the effort. Consider health and safety issues when hanging banners and considering locations for display. Never endanger your PR team. Also consider that you may be liable if the banner were to fall on a car whilst driving, resulting in an accident. It's been known to happen.

Don't forget that design-wise, your banner is only seen for a few seconds, so it needs to be punchy and to the point. Don't overcrowd it with too much information. I'd look at including the Group Name, Show Name, Venue and Dates. Include either a website or phone number for bookings.

Most importantly, when the event is over, take the banner down. There's nothing worse than seeing old banners fluttering about and you will do nothing but anger residents and councils by leaving them up for others to dispose of.

Chapter 14 - Thoughts and actions

- Think about poster placement carefully. Make your posters count.

- Make your banners punchy and remember to take them down afterwards.

15. LISTINGS

A small, but very important PR tool.

Listings are a simple way to list your auditions and productions in a number of media platforms (print, radio, and online) often at no cost.

Many groups ignore the potential of listings, but they can often draw in people who might not normally see your shows. This can be a benefit if the show you are producing isn't selling.

Like most aspects of PR, there are rules relating to listings that need to be observed. At the moment, most media outlets are cutting staff and no longer have the manpower to take your raw material and mould it into the information that they need.

So here are a few tips for taking on the challenge of getting your show listed:-

1. Identify all of the listings sources that would be suitable for your production. This should include, but is not limited to, national press, magazines, local press, radio, websites and social media, your own group newsletter, and local tourist authorities, amongst others. The key to assembling your 'master list' for contacts is keeping your eyes open and making note of any listings you see. You would be surprised just how often you encounter listings without even realising it.

2. Once you have identified your 'hit list', take a look at how listings are dealt with in each publication. Again, sending pages of information to listings services might mean that your show doesn't appear. Don't overdo it. If the person assembling the pages is overworked and under deadline pressures, they quite often won't have time to extract the relevant details if you give them way too much information. Take the time to work out the format of the listings you are approaching and then supply the relevant information with very little else. Don't be surprised if you end up sending both a press release to the editor of a publication and a separate listing to the listings editor. Receipt of a press release by the editor won't guarantee you a listing in many cases.

3. Some listings services are automated, requiring you to enter the relevant information into a website. Make sure you work out how listings need to be submitted and follow the guidelines. Nothing makes an editor more irritable than receiving information that should be sent through an automated system or that is received in the wrong format (i.e. all in UPPER CASE).

4. ALWAYS, ALWAYS, ALWAYS get someone to check over the information you are submitting. You would be amazed at just how many times listings are submitted without crucial details like a venue name, a booking number or the name of the show itself. Don't laugh, it happens more often than you would like to believe. Accuracy is everything! Always ring the booking number in your own listing to make sure it is correct. Once it is printed, you can't correct an incorrect number, and you don't want to lose a potential customer because they were unable to reach you.

5. Make sure your listings information contains the appropriate press contact on the off chance that further information is required.

6. Timing is everything! Ideally you will submit your information as far in advance as possible. Usually with listings, advance notice is not an issue. The information is received, processed and stored. A lot of listings services work months in advance, so the earlier you submit the more people are likely to see your information. Submitting a week before your show hits the stage is likely to be a complete waste of time.

As mentioned, listings are usually free and for that reason it really doesn't hurt to go to town submitting your show wherever you can. Don't shy off national listings either. Theatre enthusiasts are notorious for travelling to see shows they particularly like. List nationally if you can, what have you got to lose?

As you build a contact database for listings, you will be amazed at the numbers of sources that build up quite quickly. Media outlets will realise you aren't monitoring all of them all the time, but it's worthwhile checking each of your media sources twice a year to check that their processes or formats haven't changed. Staying aware of what's required will keep you in the good books of the listings editors and give you a better chance of scoring those all important listings.

Chapter 15 - Thoughts and actions

- Don't ignore the power of listings.

- Don't bombard the listings editor with irrelevant information.

- Make sure you are aware of deadlines and submission methods for all your potential targets.

- Get someone to check your submissions for accuracy.

- It's better to be listed everywhere. Go to town and submit to as many as you can.

16. ADVERTISING

Some things remain constant.

Many groups will always look at taking out some cheap radio commercials or a few advertisements in their local newspaper as a way of securing ticket sales. This is a time honoured technique that can have a great effect on your box office, but a few factors need to be considered before laying out any money:-

1. *Timing* - Carefully consider the timing of your advertisements. If the newspaper is weekly and published on a Wednesday, running your ad in the week of your show may prove to be a waste if your show runs Wednesday to Saturday. Some of the readers may not read the paper until the weekend rendering your ad ineffective. Timing can be a tricky proposition. You need to hit the spot at just the right time – not too early and not too late. A run of ads (or multiple insertions) may help here by spreading the message and at the same time providing brand/show re-enforcement.

2. *Add-ons* - Ad sales in many publications in the current market are down and you can sometimes score some amazing deals by haggling a bit. Don't be afraid to ask your sales rep if they can guarantee you editorial to run with your ad. Would the publication run a competition for you or mention you on their social media groups? Being a little bit cheeky can often bear fruit as sales executives struggle to hit their targets.

3. *Late space* - If ads are just too expensive for your group, don't be afraid to mention that sales executives should get in touch if they have "late space" deals to offer. Quite often publications will struggle to fill ad positions. It always pays to let it be known you may take one if the price is right. There are some great deals to be had.

4. *Position/ Placement* - Always ask where your ad will be positioned or aired. Try to secure a prominent placement if at all possible. Right hand pages are often considered to be prime positions as psychologically people tend to look at them first.

5. *Mock Up* - If you are placing a print ad, mock it up, cut it out and place it in the publication you are using. See how the ad looks when placed on the page. It's amazing how often this simple technique will engender a re-design to make your message stand out more.

6. *Misprint* - If your ad doesn't print correctly or there are problems, make a point of calling your advertising representative to lodge your disapproval immediately. You may just find yourself the beneficiary of a repeat ad or other bonus to keep you happy as a client. Be reasonable though!

7. *Ad production* - Most groups will not have the ability to produce a radio ad, so ask your local station if they can help with production as part of the package. Quite often, bringing on their expertise will help you to structure a commercial that will get you maximum results.

8. *Ask for advice* - When placing radio ads, discuss with your station what packages are available and what times they suggest you air your ad. Ask your group to indicate

what times they listen, and do some of your own research into what programmes run at what times. Would drive-time get you the best result or are you better placed in the arts programme that runs on a Sunday?

9. *Guaranteed Editorial* - Talk to your radio station about whether your ad spend can include any guaranteed interviews or promotional spots to help you promote your show.

10. *Sponsorship* - Talk to your local radio station or newspaper about part-sponsorship deals based around mutual publicity. That is, you feature an ad for them or logo on your press material and programme, in exchange for a slightly larger ad run. Don't be afraid to approach your local radio station or newspaper for a sponsorship deal. You may be able to cut the cost of advertising altogether by 'getting into bed' with your local provider.

Chapter 16 - Thoughts and actions

- Advertising is an expensive option for most groups so must be sourced and planned carefully.

- Ask the advice of experts to help you plan.

- Make your ad presentation as professional as you possibly can.

- Check, check and double check information in your ad to ensure it is correct.

- Why pay for it if you can do a deal to get it for FREE?

17. OTHER PR TECHNIQUES WORTH CONSIDERING

WALKING BILLBOARDS – USING YOUR CAST TO PROMOTE YOUR SHOW

One of the great developments that came out of musical theatre in the eighties was the explosion of merchandising relating to shows. Clothing featuring the logo of the latest show became fashion items. To a great degree that remains unchanged. Look around your rehearsal room to get an idea of just how many "Show" t-shirts your cast are wearing.

Wouldn't it be better if they were wearing a t-shirt or sweatshirt for your show?

Think about printing a garment where your show logo is prominently shown on the front. On the rear you can show dates, venue and website.

If you are really wanting your cast to show pride in their show, why not include cast names on the back as well. Nothing gets a cast more motivated than having a promotional item to wear with their name on it.

Utilising your cast as walking billboards is nothing new. It will get your show hours of free promotional exposure as they walk around doing their daily business. It will also give your cast smart promotional wear for when they are out flyering, attending interviews or working to promote the show.

SPECIAL EVENTS

Whether it be your local school or church fete, a theatre open day or any number of other occasions, make a point of looking at how you might use these events to your benefit.

Flyer teams, an information stall or a public performance, can help promote your group or production at often little or no cost. Talk to your local council, your theatre or keep an eye out in your local press for opportunities that might present themselves. But when they do, be organised and ready to pounce.

If organising a community stall, you might consider a fund-raising raffle, face painting for children or cast in character costumes as ways to make your presence interesting.

JOIN AN ASSOCIATION

In the world of amateur theatre, several associations and umbrella organisations exist that can help you to promote your shows such as NODA (www.noda.org.uk) and Little Theatre Guild (www.littletheatreguild.org).

Chapter 17 - Thoughts and actions

- Your cast can become walking advertisements for your show.

- Community events can be a great way to connect your group with potential patrons.

- Join an organisation to help you promote your work and support your endeavours.

18. GIMMICKS

*To quote the famous musical "you gotta get
a gimmick if you wanna get ahead" (Gypsy).*

Gimmicks are not the be-all and end-all of any marketing campaign, but they can certainly grab attention and bring some light relief to your PR campaign.

Gimmicks by nature can encompass a wide range of actions in relation to a PR campaign. Usually, the best way to judge the potential of a gimmick is to see if someone else has done it before and what success they had with it. That's not always to say yours won't be better, but it will give you some form of guidance. Some of the great gimmicks I've seen include:-

1. **A 'Pay What You Like' performance.**
This is exactly what it says on the tin. In an effort to fill an empty performance early in the run, audiences are invited to pay what they like for a ticket. Before you turn your noses up at this, some groups report increased takings as people give more than what is normally charged out of guilt, or to try to support the group. Either way, it tends to fill a house and if the production is good, your show gets immediate word of mouth as people can't wait to tell others about the deal they got and the show they saw. After all, there's nothing like a perceived bargain.

2. **Flash mobs.**
This is a more recent development that has arisen out of national television commercials and viral videos online.

What seems like random people in a public space, start singing a song or doing a dance routine much to the amazement of those around. Beware, these are not as easy to do as it sounds. You need to alert not only the press, but also the appropriate people of what you are intending to do, especially if it's private property. Do it right or your gimmick may end up getting you bad press. Make sure you have someone on hand to video your promotion. You can then post clips on social media sites to help promote your efforts.

3. **Special performances.**
I've seen groups hold special charity nights where you get a free programme and drink for an inflated ticket price with a charity benefitting. There's nothing new in this, but think about theming your night just to add some colour. For example, a gangster theme for *Guys and Dolls* might see audience members turn up dressed to the nines.

4. **Group booker launches.**
I wasn't overly keen to include this as a gimmick, but I realise that for many groups it would be.

This works very effectively for groups who are actively developing their group bookings of 10 or more. Potential group bookers are invited to a drink and canapé launch where they see sneak previews of a forthcoming show(s). Ticket sales people are on-hand to take bookings, with the performers feeling like they've been involved in a special night, and the potential bookers feeling you've appreciated their worth and given them something special. Don't ever underestimate the power of group bookings. It is an area that many groups ignore or avoid. It's worth the effort to gradually build your group's business. Taking advance bookings for 20% of the seats in your season can really help your bottom line and also get word of mouth going as these people ask others if they are going to the show they have already booked.

Ultimately, your gimmick is very much determined by you, but it should meet a few criteria:-

1. Will it add to your PR efforts for the show or merely detract, taking a lot of time to arrange without much return?

2. How much will it cost? Don't spend a fortune unless you can be assured of a return.

3. Is the company comfortable undertaking your gimmick? Putting people outside their comfort zones can be detrimental and their discomfort often shows. You want your company to appear happy and confident.

Chapter 18 - Thoughts and actions

- Gimmicks can be of huge benefit if thought through properly.

- Ensure that you have relevant permissions for any gimmicks planned in public.

- Are the participants comfortable with what you have planned? Appearing confident is everything.

19. EMAIL MARKETING

*The most powerful marketing medium
that every group can afford.*

When I first started doing amateur theatre in 1986, the theatre group I worked with operated a small mailing list that cost patrons a small fee to receive quarterly mailings on our shows.

This built into a free mailing list of several thousand patrons and group bookers, which allowed the group to stage seasons lasting several weeks in huge venues. Our mailing list meant that we could be sure of a healthy advance from our regular patrons months before the show opened, with special offers ensuring that those difficult to sell early shows in the season were nearly always full. Whilst it cost us to post to all of these clients, our return on the mail-out was tenfold.

How times have changed!

In today's climate, I think most patrons would laugh at the suggestion that they pay you for the privilege of being informed about your show.

That combined with the sheer cost of post means that most groups have had to adapt to modern technologies – some more successfully than others.

Email and online marketing needn't be difficult though. It operates on almost exactly the same principal and can be a far more direct means of engaging potential audiences, especially if they can buy a ticket online through a link from your email.

As with all PR and marketing, a structured approach is necessary. Think through the process first and you'll avoid a lot of costly problems further down the track.

Communication with your patrons should be thought about in phases. Try to communicate in three or four steps.

Step 1 – *Here We Go* – Announce the show is about to go on sale. Give a brief synopsis and any salient sales points about why your customers should purchase now. Securing the best seats, a early-bird discount, or the hint of a sell-out, can all work in your favour.

Step 2 – *Mid Campaign Reminder* – Tell your customer that tickets are selling well, talk about the positive press received so far, include some of your researched factoids for general interest, but most importantly present a 'call to action' such as "Don't delay – get your tickets now by visiting our website".

Step 3 – *Opening Night Imminent* – Tell your customer that certain performances are near to sell out, that the season has been extended due to popular demand, but make the message sharp and punchy. Most importantly, stress the importance of booking NOW.

Step 4 – *The Post-Opening Night Mail* – No matter how short your season, it's worth a follow-up email after opening night. Supply a social commentary of the night, mentioning local celebrities or dignitaries who attended, with pictures included if you can. You can include excerpts from reviews if you have any. Most importantly, stress that there are only a few days left to catch the show.

Like it or not, the majority of your audience will have an email account, you can't afford to ignore them.

So how do you begin?

THE BASICS

Data Protection

No matter where you are in the world, you can be reasonably assured that there will be some form of government regulation that relates to the gathering and dissemination of information via electronic means. How many times have you had the "Data Protection" trump card waived at you when trying to ascertain information? Well fear not, it's easy to jump this hurdle and as long as you stick to a few basic rules, you'll be fine.

Here in the UK, the rules relating to email marketing are regulated by the Information Commissioners Office (www. ico.gov.uk). If you need to find your local regulator, go to Google and enter Data Protection Laws and see where they direct you.

When you visit the ICO website, the basic rules relating to Data Protection are laid out in plain English. You can even take a simple online quiz to find out if you even need to register at all (http://www.ico.gov.uk/notify/self/question1. html).

In many cases, you won't need to register because you

are working within the confines of an existing customer relationship. Communication with existing patrons and interested patrons is not Spam (unsolicited email).

If you are planning to be more aggressive with your email campaigns, you may need to register, but doing so is inexpensive and relatively easy.

Don't skip this step. Take the time to look at the rules for your region. Forewarned is forearmed.

The List
So, you are starting from scratch, but don't worry.

Step 1. How big is your potential audience?
It may sound obvious, but the needs of a group playing in a local town hall will be completely different to that of a group playing a major venue for several weeks. At the core, the principal is exactly the same, but the tools you need will be slightly different. Have a think about how many people might join your email list. There are many systems available that are free if you are dealing with less than 500 people. The bigger your list gets, the more likely it is you'll need to pay to store and maintain it.

Step 2. The software.
"But can't I just email people from my Hotmail account?" I hear you asking already. You can, but it's certainly not recommended. Many Internet Service Providers block people sending large amounts of bulk email, and for anyone who has had their email blocked for suspected spamming will tell you it's a real pain.

Never fear, modern technology offers you several solutions

which will make your life so much easier and allow you to do marketing wonders.

I've included an appendix of Email Mailing sites in this book that you can use. Always look around and just think about the future. A package that is free now may charge you more in a few months when you get inundated with people wanting to be on your list. Whilst a package that might cost you a few pounds now, may stay cheap even when you have 10,000 people signed up (we should all be that lucky).

You'll also need to think about your group and the information that you want to collect. It's not just a case of collecting an email address. Modern systems allow you to capture an incredible amount of information that will allow you to target your communications like never before. When collecting data, basic information should be mandatory (Name and email address). Other information can be made optional.

Some of the suggested things you might want to find out about include:-

• The name of the person;

• Email address;

• Who they work for or the company they represent;

• Age range;

• Location;

• What type of shows do they like? (Comedy, drama, pantomime, musicals, classic shows, concerts, new writing - the choice here is endless);

• Are they interested in group bookers discounts?

• How many tickets do they normally buy when they visit the theatre?

• Are they interested in information about your benefactors programme?

• Where did they hear about the group? – Always a good one to help plan your next campaign.

• Are they interested in joining the group?

The possibilities are endless. As much as it can be tempting, don't overdo it. You don't want to scare away your potential patron. Keep it simple.

Once you have this Sign Up Questionnaire sorted you are ready to go. Most online systems will give you the option of installing a Mailing List Sign Up Box on your website. Talk to your webmaster and get their help with this. It's not complicated, but best left to someone who knows what they are doing. But do it you must – you'll be surprised how many people will sign up this way.

Step 3. Names, names, names.
In order for people to sign up, you need to get the ball rolling. Let people know that you are offering a new service and see how you go. You can use enticements like discount offers, special performances, behind-the-scenes

information and anything else you can think of that might excite a potential patron. Be careful to examine the rules relating to 'Opt-In' sign ups. Your software provider will usually have a help section that explains this. In its most basic form people must give you permission to add their names to your list. Blasting thousands of unsuspecting recipients is SPAM. Using professional software will give recipients the opportunity to 'unsubscribe' from your list easily and effectively if they so wish. Just follow the rules and you will be fine.

Start with all of your company members. Ask everyone in your group to sign up. The software system you use will usually offer the chance to contact potential list members just by entering their details. An email is then sent out offering them the opportunity to register. Ask your members to send the invitation out to anyone they know who comes to see them in shows and so forth. We've talked before about viral marketing and this operates on the same word of mouth principal, but it's a great way to start getting the right people on your list. You'll be surprised how quickly your list starts to get populated and the numbers begin to grow.

You can pre-set your software to send out a welcome message for each new sign up. Use this opportunity to say thank you for signing up and ask them to recommend the mailing list to any friends they know who might be interested.

You'll soon be ready to send out your first email, but be careful, your first communication is important. You have the trust of your audience, don't lose it by sending out irrelevant messages. Keep your message targeted, focused, interesting and make it reflect the way you want your group to be seen in public. This is not a joke being emailed around the office. It is an official communication from your company.

Step 4. Talking to your list.

Once again, most software systems will offer you a range of ready made templates that will make your email look professionally produced. You can usually upload pictures, change the fonts and really make your email look like a million quid.

Plan your email in advance. Decide amongst the group whether you are looking to communicate once a month, or at whatever frequency you like, and try to stick to it. Inundating your contact list with email can turn people off and result in them unsubscribing. If you regularly send out an email at a particular time of the month, it won't take long before people on your list start to expect it and respond with enthusiasm.

There are several benefits that come with using one of the email software packages. These include:-

• Clients have the ability to unsubscribe or change their details by clicking the link at the bottom of the email without needing to hassle you. Your list can basically maintain itself. This functionality is also one of the key factors to Data Protection. If people want to leave your list they must be able to do so easily.

• When you send a mail-out, within a few hours you can get instant access to a range of information including how many people have read your email, who they are, if they have clicked on any of the links contained in the email.

• The system will also tell you how many emails have come back with wrong contact information and allow you to remove them.

• Your emails are well-presented and can also be viewed online through a web link.

• Some modern systems also allow you to post your newsletter to Facebook and Twitter, giving you even bigger coverage.

The work that you did earlier setting up your list criteria should now allow you to contact only those people who like Drama, perhaps those that want news of group discounts, becoming a member of your theatre group, even people who would be interested in sponsoring your show or buying an advertisement in your programme (Did you think of that one earlier in this chapter?)

It's also possible to sell advertising space on your email blasts. If you have a local restaurant near your theatre, why not ask them if they'd like to place some text and a photo on your next email to encourage pre-theatre dining? You're providing a service for your audience and helping to cover the small costs associated with running the list. I've even seen one group provide an Amazon affiliate link to the Broadway Cast Recording of the show they are staging, on the chance people might like to listen to the songs before. That affiliate link also pays the group a percentage of sales made, so it's a win win. For further information visit https://affiliate-program.amazon.co.uk/

Back Up

Be warned – no software is infallible. No software company is immune from going bust, so it pays to explore the software and familiarise yourself with the list back-up function. It should be relatively easy to save all the data collected as an Excel spreadsheet, or in some other format, so you don't lose everything if something goes wrong.

Treat your list audience with respect, provide a helpful service and you'll find it will grow quickly. The rewards will start to become obvious.

Chapter 19 - Thoughts and actions

- Email communication with your audience is a must for every theatre group no matter how small.

- Don't assume the Data Protection Act doesn't apply to you. Make sure you check your status.

- Strategically build your mailing list. There's no point having 7000 people on your list if only 50 respond.

- Gather information appropriate to your marketing campaigns.

- Plan your audience communication strategy.

- Make sure you back-up the list.

20. YOUR WEBSITE

Your calling card to millions of people.

The more that I work with amateur groups across the UK, the more I am amazed that so many do not have an online presence in the form of their own website.

There are three common arguments that I hear again and again to explain the lack of online presence:-

1.   It costs too much.
2.   It's too complicated.
3.   We don't need one.

In response, my answers to these statements would be:-

1.   No, it doesn't.
2.   No, it's not.
3.   Yes, you most certainly do.

I know I keep coming back to this, but you need to identify with your audience. Chances are they are all online, they have most certainly purchased tickets for a movie or show online, booked a holiday online, talked to friends via email or have Facebook profiles. The media you talk to will primarily communicate via email, and pictures will be sent via email or through an online transfer service like Dropbox (www.dropbox.com).

With all this in mind, why wouldn't they expect to be able to find information about your group online through your own dedicated website?

There is no doubt that in the early days of the World Wide Web, setting up a website was a costly affair, but now sites can be established cheaply.

THERE IS NOW LITTLE OR NO EXCUSE FOR A GROUP NOT TO HAVE THEIR OWN DEDICATED PRESENCE ONLINE.

So what are the key components for any amateur theatre website:-

• *Information about the history of your group*. This could include a list of past productions.

• *Contacts for your group* - Whether this is one central email address or a list of email contacts for various departments, you need to ensure that your email is checked and responses made daily. There is nothing more frustrating than being unable to reach a company with an urgent media request.

• *Information about your current show and your forthcoming productions* - This should include the show logo, venue information, times and dates, prices, cast and production team listings and booking information.

• *Photo Gallery* – Galleries of photos from previous productions.

• *Media Centre* – Why not set up a page that has current press and news releases? Copies of press clippings relating to the group and links to high resolution pictures (see

Photography - Chapter 12) that can be easily downloaded for the media to use. This will prove to be very popular with journalists increasing your chances of editorial coverage.

• *Support* – Set up a page for potential sponsors of people wishing to support you financially. Show people what's on offer and make it look attractive to become involved.

• *Taking Part* – Information on how people can join your group.

• *Links* – A page of online links to useful sites. This can include sponsors, suppliers, support bodies like NODA or The Little Theatre Guild, media supporters, and other theatre sites. Ask other groups to link to your site, it helps raise your visibility and makes it easier to find you if someone is looking.

• *Mailing List* – Make it easy for patrons to join your email list via your website.

Think about your site content as if you were the customer. What would you expect to find if you were looking for information about your company?

The Domain Name.
One of the keys to getting a good listing in search engines like Google is held in the domain name you pick for your group. It's worth owning your own domain name. Imagine how incensed you might get if someone else had your group's name registered for the web?

There is great debate about how search engines use domain names to list websites. Previously groups have been advised to try to avoid registering acronyms like www.daodcs. co.uk. It was thought that registering full names like www. dundasamateuroperaticsociety.co.uk would get you better search engine placement. Ultimately, the way that search engines work is subject to constant change, so choose the domain that you feel is best for you.

We Can't Afford It.

As with social networking, it's worth talking to some of the younger members of your group. Chances are some of them have built their own website and would be happy to help you build a society site. If that's not an option, there are several pre-packed deals you can take advantage of.

Sites such as www.wix.com, www.webeden.co.uk, or www.moonfruit.com can help you build a simple, but polished site. You will never get a site for free (unless you have a benefactor who is web savvy) so think about your site as a revenue raiser not just a cost. Many hosting packages now include ample space for a website sufficient to most groups needs. Just ensure that you are not tied to a complicated domain name in the process. You must be able to apply your own domain name to your site, otherwise avoid it like the proverbial plague.

Many groups sell advertising banner slots on their websites. You'll be surprised how many local restaurants or other small business will be prepared to part with a few pounds to advertise their businesses to your members and audiences. £10-£15 for a banner for a month or two on your website will help you cover any hosting costs.

You could in fact turn your website into an income generating part of your theatre company. There is nothing to limit the amount of advertising or business links that you could sell to potential clients.

Local businesses, restaurants in-and-around your theatre, local cab firms, radio stations, music or bookstores, amongst others, provide a ready-made group of companies who might appreciate the audience flow-on from one of your shows.

The bottom line though is that your website must be included in your cost of marketing. In exactly the same way that you produce flyers and posters, your website is an important part of your marketing and can't be ignored.

Online Ticketing.

Many groups also offer online ticket sales facilities via their websites. Whether you like it or not, in a short time, any group not selling tickets online will be at a distinct disadvantage and will be quickly overtaken by rivals who do. As a PR team, I would be recommending to your committee or implementing online sales as soon as possible. Groups can no longer afford to lose ticket sales through inaccessible ticket buying procedures, that in many cases, date back to the Fifties.

Many groups complain that the cost of selling tickets online is prohibitive. It's time to realise that you now need to factor in the cost of selling online as one of the basic costs of doing business. Denying your audience this convenience is no longer an option. You will watch your audiences dwindle rather than enjoying sold out houses. Many years ago, most groups couldn't see the need to accept credit cards and learnt the hard way as ticket sales declined. Online ticketing is the next major turning point for our industry and you must be onboard to survive.

Time is a most precious commodity and having caught the attention of a potential patron, you want them to buy a ticket as quickly and conveniently as possible. Why spend hours attracting patrons only to have them lose interest because tickets can only be purchased by physically going to an address which is miles away, or only being able to book by phone during restricted hours. Most people don't have time in busy schedules anymore. Make it simple!

There's no doubt that technology continues to march ever onward, leaving some early adopters with huge benefits as the technology comes of age and the latecomers trying to play catch up. During the course of preparing this book and articles for Amateur Stage Magazine, I canvassed a number of groups across the country and have included their feedback in this chapter, as it seemed indicative of the community as a whole.

I've previously been quietly cajoling groups to look at online sales methods, but now I'm prepared to make this prediction. If your immediate competitor offers online sales and you don't (and by online sales I'm talking about picking your seat allocation and buying on the spot – not just a ticket request form) you can easily expect to be overtaken by them, and in some cases, be out of business in the next few years. Not selling online will be tantamount to writing a death notice for your company. Harsh words, but I believe them to be true.

Where in the past, the much-venerated ticket secretary was the cornerstone of the ticketing operation, an electronic solution is now available that is functional 24 hours a day,

7 days a week, gives patrons greater choices and takes payment instantly.

This problem was best summed up by one group, who said: "We don't yet sell tickets online. We have a wonderful booking secretary who runs our box office almost single-handed. She takes bookings by telephone and in person during the run of a production and the Sundays running up to a production. She knows most of our audience by name and is a great PR asset. We are considering going online, but then we would lose her services: she is not technically adept. One of our local theatres uses an online booking system run by a local professional theatre and we have to pay a booking fee. For us, this is a no win situation."

Another group commented: "The box offices in the three theatres we produce in are all run by rather elderly volunteers with extremely limited box office hours (a couple of hours a day at most - and never out of normal working hours).

"Our experience has increasingly been that as the theatres have added credit card booking facilities, personal callers and telephone bookings are taking a very long time and consequently nobody can get through to them! (Weird how this happens in all three theatres, but there you go!). This week we are producing the Mikado and my phone has been like a hotline of complaints against the theatre box office staff as the phone is permanently engaged.

"We have taken an allocation of seats and sell them online, adding more seats as we sell out. This has had several effects; it has:-

1) stopped people hassling me about not being able to get through to theatre box offices;

2) increased ticket sales as we can bypass long waits for tickets;

3) allowed us to put in price promotions for tickets - something that theatres don't like doing;

4) given us a more professional, personalised sales page.

For most groups though, the big decision about going online with ticketing comes down to one thing - COST!

"Many groups thought that the percentage fees charged by both the software providers when combined with the credit card companies were prohibitive. Some groups solved this problem by adopting a split system where they footed the bill for a portion of the fees, but charged a small booking fee to patrons, thus sharing the fees involved.

"What did become clear from our survey of both venues and audiences was that audience expectations were out of synch with what groups believed.

"Many patrons we surveyed were prepared to support local amateur groups, but found that doing so was more and more complicated, time consuming and difficult. It was perhaps best summed up by a patron who said 'if my local group allowed me to buy online, select the seat I wanted and do so at a time that best suited me, I'd happily pay a little bit extra for the privilege. I don't have time to mess around.' This was an attitude reflected in 90% of the responses received. Another commented: 'I'm used to paying a booking fee for the cinema and professional theatre, so if a booking fee was added to an amateur group it wouldn't turn me off buying a ticket."

So, do the benefits of online selling outweigh the downside? Let's look at some of the pros and cons of selling tickets online:-

The Pros:-

1. Tickets are available for purchase 24/7.

2. Tickets are paid for in advance – tickets left for collection and payment are a thing of the past.

3. Usually customers are able to select where they wish to sit, giving them greater choice.

4. In most cases, generating e-tickets reduces costs to the group in not having to print huge quantities of paper tickets.

5. Statistics related to sales are usually available allowing your marketing team to evaluate sales promotions to see what works and how your audience buy their tickets for future planning.

6. Drastically reduces man-hours normally put in by volunteers.

7. Patrons don't need to leave their homes to buy a ticket.

8. Anyone with a credit or debit card can purchase – no cheque book necessary.

The Cons:-

1. Some patrons are not online.

2. Eliminates the human face of the transaction in the form of the ticket secretary in many transactions.

3. Cost of the system and card fees must be considered.

4. The impression that you need to be overly 'tech-savvy' to run the system.

5. Money from sales kept by a third-party until after the production finishes. (Although this is not the case with all systems).

Whilst there may be other pros and cons, these were the main points raised by the groups responding to our research request.

It was interesting to note the number of groups who had shackled together their own "online ticketing systems". I use that term loosely as most are just glorified methods of accepting a credit card payment. Whilst many found such makeshift systems served their purposes, others used such systems to illustrate how online ticketing didn't work. Whilst use of Paypal accounts to accept payments online was innovative, I came to the conclusion that comparisons of this type of system were ill-advised, as they did not reflect a true online ticketing system.

Perhaps one of the most reflective summation statements came from Julian Cound at Darlington Operatic Society, who surmised: "It is clear that online sales are a must for any amateur society wanting to move forward, not necessarily as the only way to purchase tickets, but as an additional service. In selling tickets for your productions, you are offering a service and, as in any service industry, the customer is king. You have to put a system in place that makes it as easy as possible for your potential paying customer to part with their hard earned cash. People are getting more and more used to choosing where they sit when buying theatre tickets, so this also has to be a strong consideration. Taking away the fact that cheques will soon be obsolete (although other payment methods may replace them), you simply have to ask yourself how many 'young people' have a cheque book now and how many ever send a letter in the post? Like it or not, our next generation of audience are more likely to purchase online and expect a confirmation of order via email. By not offering the ability to purchase online you are losing out on a potentially huge audience base."

It is probably worth looking at your audiences and wondering who they might be in five years time. If the amateur and fringe theatre community don't move forward with modern technology, we could soon see our audiences diminish further as archaic ticketing systems are rejected by modern audiences with busy lives. Future developments include the ability to purchase using electronic tablet devices and mobile phone applications.

TOP TIPS FOR SELLING ONLINE

1. Invest the time to find a decent ticketing system that works for you. Properly developed systems make it easier for your customer and for your group, by making the experience as easy as possible for all concerned. The less

manpower involved, the better off you are.

2. Make a commitment to being an online provider. Don't just put the worst seats in the house on sale online. If you are only putting a small allocation online, make sure you allocate a mixture of seats in all price brackets and monitor uptake, placing more on sale if necessary. It's hard to sell a lot of tickets online if the available choice is poor.

3. Advertise the fact that you can buy online. Don't forget your website is your shop front to a world of possibilities. Make it as attractive as possible and encourage people to buy online. Younger audiences use QR Codes, Twitter and Facebook – make sure you tell people to buy online using these methods.

4. If you are producing a season of shows, put all your season on sale at once. Some patrons will see others shows you are presenting while purchasing and may be tempted to book on impulse.

5. Monitor your system to keep an eye on how you are selling. Take note of sales spikes and seek to find out what caused them. That interview at midnight on your local radio station might just see people going online to book. Don't lose a sale because your telephone booking person is asleep!

6. If you are going to charge a booking fee, be transparent about it. Most consumers accept the need for such a fee but object to finding out after they get to the checkout as the budget airlines found out!

7. Find out if your system allows you to database buyers

email addresses. Having the ability to instantly email everyone who bought tickets for your last show when you are putting your next show on sale can be a valuable tool.

WHAT SOME OF THE GROUPS SAID

"We are totally satisfied with the results. Over 70% of sales were via the link provided on our own website and we have been able to drastically reduce the time our own box office has been open - a considerable saving in time for our volunteers. It has eliminated the losses from "no-shows" which is very important to us as we now have 100% occupancy for most of our late week shows. We still provide a postal service for those of our patrons who are not internet aware, but many of them use friends and family to book. It is really useful to be able to provide a 24/7 service to our customers, and analysis of purchase information backs this up, showing tickets sales made around the clock." *Weymouth Drama Club.*

"I acquired the privileged role of Business Manager two years ago. With that role also came the ticket secretary role. Having successfully run my own business for five years, I was a little surprised to see that neither the society or theatre were able to offer online ticket sales in an already lucrative market. In my eyes, we were missing out. Since then, we have developed an online website which links to Ticketsource. The 2011 pantomime season has seen the highest usage for sales - helped by the fact the Ticketsource link, QR code to our website and regular online marketing activity through Facebook and Twitter, really did help push online sales. We really have gone online! As a result, the 2011 pantomime season was our best ever for sales for the last ten years." *Workington & District Amateur Musical Society.*

"We use Nortech Software & have done for 3 years now. As well as using it for our in-house drama group, we also use it to sell all tickets to all events at our theatre and find it very useful. We also have the online facility for people to purchase online, which is used more than over the phone now. I would say 85% of tickets are sold online rather than in-person or over the phone". *Garth Spann. Avenue Theatre.*

"We are an amateur society and operate a 180-seater theatre, plus an 80-seater studio. We sell about 70% of our tickets online nowadays - and rising!" *Queen Mother Theatre, Hitchin, Herts.*

Chapter 20 - Thoughts and actions

- The website as an audience (not to mention a media) interface is now a must have for any theatre group.

- Your website must be kept current and up-to-date with clear contacts listed.

- Facebook does not substitute for a website – EVER!

- Online ticketing is now a must for every theatre group with the costs of sales factored in. No group can afford empty seats by not catering to this market.

21. THE IMMEDIACY OF SOCIAL NETWORKING

It's so much more than most of us realise.

In recent years, the global reach of social networking platforms has expanded to a point where it can no longer be ignored as a means for publicising your group and your show.

The two major benefits offered by social networking sites like Twitter and Facebook are that they offer immediacy of contact and the services they offer are usually free of charge.

Don't just rush into social media though, thinking that it is a quick and easy way of promoting your show. That attitude has left many sorely disappointed. Like any publicity mechanism it needs a structured approach and thought before attack.

In this chapter, I am addressing some of the important factors relating to social networking. It is not a "How To" guide. Can I suggest an investment in a "Dummies Guide" will equip you with all the knowledge you need to run a social networking account.

Social networking does offer your group an opportunity to bring one of the younger, more enthusiastic members of your company onto your PR committee. If you find the concept of social networking difficult, enlist the support of a younger member who will usually be well versed in how such systems work.

We would suggest that at the time of writing, Twitter (www.twitter.com) and Facebook (www.facebook.com) are the two major platforms that warrant your time and offer the best effort to potential return ratio.

Before launching into social networking, there are a few things to consider:-

1. Immediacy.

Many West End shows are now realising that their expensive publicity campaigns and launches are now being trumped by casual postings from cast, crew or staff. Casual quips can quickly find their way onto Twitter and once done it is very difficult to stop them.

Stop to think about what you are going to post to social networks. Get your Tweet right and you'll find it will be re-Tweeted many times. Forget a vital detail and it is unlikely many will re-Tweet your correction.

2. Economy.

Be economical with your contact. You need to establish the right balance between you and your audience. As a magazine, Amateur Stage finds that people are keen to get a wide spread of information on a regular basis. As a theatre company, be economical so that your message isn't lost in an avalanche of information. This forms a part of point 3.

3. Consumer Engagement.

Before diving into Twitter, have a think about how you want your customers to interact with you. You need to remember that consumers aren't necessarily eager or ready to buy tickets from you at all times. So while you may be interested in promoting an offer or a product, doing so over and over again is likely to alienate your customer base.

Many groups we have encountered online use Twitter and Facebook as nothing more than an efficient way to tell people about rehearsals. Twitter can be so much more than that. The ultimate aim should be to provide value to your customers and community. When someone chooses to follow you on Twitter, it's a sign of trust and not an open invitation to be bombarded with irrelevant information. Think about the possible uses for your social media accounts. Posting pictures from auditions and rehearsals, publication of interesting factoids, sales updates, and rehearsal updates, can all help to build momentum leading up to opening night.

With Twitter, don't be afraid to support other theatre companies in your area. Re-tweet information about their shows and ask them to do the same for you. In short though, do unto others as you would have them do unto you.

Twitter and Facebook shouldn't always be about the hard sell. Start talking to your audiences. Engage them in a conversation. Ask questions. Make them feel a part of the process. Gauge their opinions and thoughts. Getting people talking about you is every bit as important as pushing ticket sales.

Who Controls The Message?
Perhaps the most important part of Social Networking is who controls the primary message. The power of your message can quickly come unstuck when the old adage of

"too many cooks" comes into play.

Your PR committee needs to agree the plan and implement it on time. Having three or four people dipping their fingers in the pie will prove confusing. If you have an eager group who all want to help with social networking, then allocate tasks. For instance, one person can handle the re-tweeting of messages and following people back on Twitter; one person can work on actively recruiting more followers on Facebook and yet another can ensure that important posts are uploaded to your social media accounts.

Who Are You Talking To?
Sad to say that many amateur groups on Facebook and Twitter use their accounts for nothing other than advising rehearsal times. This is an extreme waste of the power of the networks.

Perhaps the best use of Facebook I've seen had a group set up a public site for their company and a private group for cast and crew.

The private group allows the cast to banter amongst themselves, arrange social functions and swap scheduling details (out of sight of the general public). Setting up a private group on Facebook is easy to do, the private option is presented when setting up your group. The group administrator can then invite people to join.

The public group allows the company to communicate a direct message with its potential audiences.

Set it and forget it.
Sad to say Facebook and Twitter are littered with amateur

theatre group accounts that have been set up and then abandoned. I've seen Facebook groups with three members which is just crazy.

Running a Twitter account or a Facebook account takes time. Social networking relies on critical mass to make the network function. You can't have a social network with one person. Networks rely on many people to post information and refer other people who might be your potential audience.

There are a few basic steps that you need to undertake:-

1. Once you have set up a Twitter or Facebook account, tell every member of your group and every friend that you have, that you are online and invite them to join you.

2. When you finish casting a show, make sure every cast member is following you online.

3. Put your social networking profile names in your programmes, on flyers, posters and on your website. Make it easy for anyone to follow your social network.

4. Sit down and seek out rights holders, members of the press, media, your suppliers, other local groups and any organisation or individual who might be interested in your company or forthcoming production. For instance, it's not unreasonable to find groups following Alan Ayckbourn if they are about to stage *Woman In Mind*. The possibilities are literally endless.

5. Find media pages (such as *Amateur Stage, Fourthwall Magazine* or *Fringe Review*) and ensure that you regularly

post your show updates. If you are staging a show that has recently enjoyed a West End run, see if it is possible to post information about your show on their Facebook wall, thus contacting any die-hard fans of the show who might be interested in your production.

6. Post occasional photos or copies of your posters and flyers to your social network account. You will be amazed at how many people will share your images to their friends. Well selected visuals are powerful and can embed your show in the brain of anyone who sees your postings. Social networking can offer one of the best forms of positive re-enforcement on an almost daily basis for any show or group.

7. Make sure that your social networking postings are positive, concise and upbeat. Be encouraging, not pessimistic! If you saw the following message: "Buy a ticket for *Death Of A Salesman* now because sales are awful and we may not make it to opening night if we don't have your support", would you buy a ticket?

You might try: "Don't forget to book your seats for *Death Of A Salesman*. This bustling pop opera storms into a theatre near you next week. This classic play by Arthur Miller is not to be missed".

8. Get people to 'like' your Facebook page or 'follow' you on Twitter. Promote competitions to help you attract new members. Offer small prizes or incentives to make their association more attractive. Perhaps giveaway the cast album to the show you are presenting or work in conjunction with a local restaurant to provide dinner for two. Try to avoid giving away tickets though. Why give away that which you are hoping to sell!

Chapter 21 - Thoughts and actions

- Social media represents one of the newest and best ways to promote your show without it costing a penny.

- Social media isn't an easy answer. Like any PR it requires planning and thought.

- Social media isn't about the hard sell. It's about engaging your customer in conversation.

- Use social media to get feedback as well as to promote.

- Social media requires constant attention and effort to grow a potential audience.

22. QR CODES

An amazing jumble of information.

You've no doubt seen them on posters, in magazines and on all manner of advertising material, but did you know what they were?

There's no doubt that technology marches ahead at breathtaking speed these days. You no sooner get your mind around one new piece of technology and you are confronted with another which usually supersedes the first.

So it was, that I seemed to have missed completely the introduction of what I would later learn was called a QR Code or *Quick Response Code.*

There's no doubt you will have seen these odd little dotted squares around town on all sorts of media, but did anyone tell you what they were and how to use them? I daresay probably not. How many people think that you take a picture of them with your camera phone and something magical happens? Well not quite.

It was only that on showing a friend a flyer mock-up I was about to print that I was confronted with the question that inspired this chapter: "Why don't you have a QR Code?".

Not wanting to look stupid, I dashed home and Googled this term to find out just what I was missing. It was a revelation!

In it's most potted form, a QR Code (short for Quick Response code) is an advanced type of barcode. Rather than just being one dimensional like the barcodes used in supermarkets and stores, a QR Code is two dimensional. The QR Code was first created by a subsidiary of Toyota as a way of tracking vehicles during the manufacturing process. The code was ideal because it could literally store vast amounts of information and was incredibly fast to read.

So what are the benefits of QR Codes? Well, they are many and varied, but for me, they win hands down as a way of gathering information for later review. How many times have you been out and about and seen a poster or advertisement for something that is of interest? Without access to pen or paper you note the website or details, and then promptly forget them as you work your way through a busy day. With a smart phone loaded with a QR Code reader, you could simply scan the code (it takes seconds), save the details in your phone and move on with the confidence of reviewing the information later at your leisure.

In so far as amateur theatre or indeed any business is concerned, QR Codes are a marketing godsend for one very specific reason. The technology to read them and create them is absolutely 100% FREE!! Having dashed home from my meeting, Googled the term, visited a website and downloaded a reader from the Apple App Store, it took me all of twenty minutes to have created my first QR Code and placed it on my flyer. It was *that* simple!

Most QR Codes when scanned will simply take you to a website, but you can include all manner of data including links to Google Maps, SMS messages, You Tube video links, Facebook links, email messages and it can even add an event date and details into your phone's diary system.

Just think about how powerful QR Codes could be. Your potential audience could see one of your posters in the street and simply scan the code and instantly have show information, dates, venue information and a link to buy tickets transferred to their phone. Without hassle, or having to chase after a flyer, you have provided them with everything they need to book a ticket instantly. When we look for ways to improve the customer experience when booking to see a show, this surely has to rank as one of the greatest developments ever.

Okay, the one big downside at the moment is that you need to have a smartphone to take advantage of the technology, but it's only a matter of time before this technology is standard. At a time when we need to increase our audience numbers, can we afford to shy away from this free technology?

I know that as far as I am concerned, this is a technology I intend on embracing on multiple levels. I'd certainly challenge every group out there to do the same. What have you got to lose?

HOW TO GET YOUR OWN QR CODES

1. Visit the App Store on your smartphone and search for 'QR Code'. The store should offer you several free apps that will read QR Codes. When you start up one of these apps,

you simply point your camera at the QR Code and *hey presto* – the magic happens.

2. To generate your QR Code, just visit one of several sites on the internet. I've used and can recommend www.qrstuff. com, www.qurify.com and www.qrcode.kaywa.com. Just follow the easy instructions and within minutes you have a QR Code that you can put onto anything you like.

WHERE TO USE THEM

Some of the places I've spotted QR Codes include:-

- Flyers
- Posters
- T-shirts
- Theatre Programmes
- On Chocolates
- Post It Notes
- Envelopes
- Business Cards
- Treasure Hunt Clues
- Business Cards

Chapter 22 - Thoughts and actions

- QR Codes are simple to obtain and apply.

- Through mobile phone technology, they offer audiences quick links with information about your show.

- QR Codes can literally be applied to anything.

23. FILMING AND YOUR SHOW

*Video can be a blessing or a curse. Use
it wisely and with permission.*

Times are changing and the way that shows are promoted
are too. Many theatre fans will be aware that more and more
West End and professional shows are moving online as a
way of promoting their shows to wider audiences. Video
clips resembling Hollywood film trailers now promote just
about every show in London's West End and on Broadway.

The process of handling this correctly isn't complicated but
has to be handled correctly to avoid the pitfalls of a legal
breach of contract. Here are some basic do's and don'ts and
a few misnomers that groups need to understand.

DON'T
• Take someone else's clip and stick your groups name and
dates on the end. No matter how hard you wish, Nathan
Lane is not going to be starring in your production of *The
Producers*. If you are going to produce a clip it must be your
own content.

• Don't create a clip and then use the cast album for the
show to provide the musical backing. Whilst you have
permission to stage the show, you don't have permission
to effectively steal someone else's recording. Websites
such as You Tube can identify content from its database of
recordings – it will notify the copyright holder and you will
be prosecuted.

• Make a video recording of your show unless you have permission. "The video is for our archive" is not a valid excuse.

DO

• Approach your publicity plans professionally. Talk to your rights holders and ask what is allowable given the license you hold. Most American musicals allow groups a 'fair usage allowance' for publicity footage. Using small clips of a show can be allowed in some cases, but ask first and be prepared to abide by the decision given.

• If approved, put together a clip that looks professional. Given software that is available on many domestic computers nowadays such as iMovies on iMacs, it is possible to produce a professional looking clip. Ask some of the younger members of your group if the technology is beyond your grasp. Chances are, they know exactly what to do. Look at other professional clips to get a feel for how to make yours look amazing. Low budget, or no budget, needn't mean low quality.

• Ensure that your clip contains any contractual billing as advised by your rights holder.

• Once you have permission and made your clip, upload it to You Tube or Vimeo and start telling everyone you know. The ability for you to get your message out to thousands of people using viral marketing means you could access a whole new audience.

• Show your website, Facebook and Twitter link on your clip.

MISNOMERS

• Many groups believe that videoing a show and making copies for everyone in the group is allowed. In most cases it isn't. Check with your rights holder. With some shows you can now pay a video fee to get appropriate permission, but you need to ask.

• You can't just copy an existing clip online and add your information to it. This is a breach of copyright and as we said earlier a clip with a West End star in it is misleading in the least and an offence at worst.

• Don't just follow what others have done. Just because *xyz group* have posted a promo video for their show, doesn't mean they have acquired permission. Always make your own enquiries just in case. If you secure your own permission, you are in the clear. Never Assume!

Chapter 23 – Thoughts and actions

• Original content is a must.

• Get permission from the rights holder.

• Use film sparingly – make your clip about 3-4 minutes in length.

24. SPONSORSHIP

*Reduce your production costs and
gain a corporate friend.*

Whilst sponsorship is not normally in the remit of the PR team, I've included this 'rough guide' in the hope it may help. Regardless of whether the PR team helps to source and negotiate sponsorship, they will have extensive dealings with sponsors in helping to promote their involvement.

In these tough economic times, many groups across the UK are looking for ways to help access extra income to keep them afloat. Many will look to sponsorship as the answer to their problems, but do groups fully understand how to take best advantage of sponsorship or even how to access sponsorship funds?

Let's dismiss the biggest myth first.

Companies do not just hand out large amount of cash to theatre groups without incentive or some form of return. In order to be successful with sponsorship, it is important that you treat it like any professional business deal. A sponsor will respect this.

Assemble a group of people to help your group achieve sponsorship success. Ideally, about three or four people. They should be literate, well-presented and above all, be able to think creatively. Often the best solutions and approaches come from outside the box, so to speak.

This group can then liaise with other committees to make your sponsorship dreams come true.

So let's begin.

1. Who can we aproach for sponsorship?

Often your most supportive sponsors will be closer to hand than you think. Firstly, it's a good idea to ask your members to fill out an information form on a regular basis. Ask members really basic questions, such as where they work, do they know people at any major companies who might be interested in programme advertising or sponsorship? You will often be surprised that you have a sponsor under your very nose. I'm not advocating hassling members because they work at big companies, but it's worth asking the question to see what possibilities exist. Sometimes companies have community funds which they issue to groups that staff are involved in.

Take a look around your area and see what businesses are based nearby. Have a think about how those businesses might benefit from an association with your group. There are many ways that companies can link to your group and it's your job to discover what those may be.

Grab a copy of any local business or telephone directories and find contact details for any local business groups like your local Lions Club. Go through these guides and make a list of possible sponsors. These guides can be helpful as there may be companies that you have not thought of. But don't be impatient. This is a process. Keep thinking and compiling a hit list of possible sponsors.

If you are using a professional venue to stage your

shows, don't be afraid to talk to management about your sponsorship needs. They may know someone who wants to help, but can't be utilised by the venue themselves. Don't think that it will come to you, quite often you will need to prompt management for them to think of your needs.

Take a look around at which companies are sponsoring community groups and other theatre groups in your area. Maybe the answer lies with those businesses, or possibly with their competition. If one business is achieving positive results from sponsorship, you can be assured that their competitors will be interested in knowing how they can get some of the action.

Do some lateral thinking. Sponsorship doesn't always have to be in the form of cash. Does your group have any needs, or do you use certain supplies that are costly and chew up your budget? Think about things like hardware supplies for sets and props, office consumables, phone bills, electricity costs, or advertising costs, etc.

2. What can you offer a sponsor?
This part of the equation can often be as time-consuming as compiling your list of potential sponsors. As a group, you need to consider what tangible benefits you can offer a potential sponsor.

Potential benefits include things like:-

• Tickets to your productions;

• Meet and greet functions with your cast and crew;

• Special VIP areas in your foyer during performances with drinks;

• Free advertising in programme;

• Corporate logos on posters, flyers and even on the tickets themselves;

• Venue signage;

• Access to mailing lists - can you include a flyer for your sponsor in your next mail out? If you mail out tickets, can you include something from your sponsor? Perhaps you can even mention your sponsor on the ticket itself.

The possibilities here are endless. It's important not to close your mind to them. More often than not, the sponsor won't realise what possibilities exist and will have their eyes opened when you present a list of thoughts that might appeal.

Be aware that your biggest asset is your group itself. Even the smallest of drama groups impact on a relatively large number of people. Count your members, the number of family members associated with each member, the number of people who see your shows, the number of flyers and posters you print, how many people read about your shows in the local press, and how many people view your website. This number soon amounts to hundreds, if not thousands, of people who can affect the goodwill that is directed towards a sponsor.

This goodwill is your greatest asset. Think of the youth theatre group, I knew, that was actually sponsored by a used car business. Being based in a small town, they offered special deals for group members when it was time for them to purchase their first car. They not only got great business out of it, but tremendous goodwill from the families because of the care they took with the customers whose group they had supported.

THE WRITTEN PROPOSAL

Let's Get Started
The first rule of sponsorship proposals is that each one should be individually written and structured towards its recipient. Of course, there are some basics that can be duplicated, but in 99% of cases the proposal will succeed or fail based on the individual approach and the customised offer.

Ideally, a written approach should be no longer than 3 - 4 pages, anything longer and you risk being filed for future reference, or binned.

Use this basic guide for your written proposal:-

Introduction.
This should be a maximum of two paragraphs explaining who you are (some information about your group) and what you are seeking sponsorship for. Keep the information crisp and to the point, don't embellish!

The Project.
Put together two to three reasonably detailed paragraphs about the project, expanding on your introduction. Discuss important factors such as the size of your audience, the participants in the project, and your geographic catchment area amongst other things.

Sponsorship Benefits.

This can be an exhaustive list. It's generally best to select and quantify say 10-15 things that you can offer sponsors. Most importantly, each item should have a value attached to it. Things you could include are:-

Tickets.

You can offer your sponsor a certain number of tickets to your show (eg. Ten Complimentary 'A' Reserve Tickets to our opening night on 4th August valued at £200). Select a reasonable number and then offer extra tickets for a reduced rate. This could help increase your sales and get new people to see your show.

Programme Advertising.

Advertising in your show programme can be a great way to mass promote your sponsor. Again, add a value to this. Regardless, there should be some mention of your production sponsors in your programme, even in a most basic listing style format.

Venue Signage.

Can you place a banner or signage for your sponsor in the venue in a prominent place?

Logo on Advertising.

Place your sponsors corporate logo on EVERY item you distribute advertising your show. This can include newspaper ads, flyers, posters, press releases, or a banner on your website, to name just a few. This type of promotion gets your sponsors name out to a lot of people. Under this point, it is worth breaking down the type of promotion you intend to do, and don't be afraid to mention quantities for your print and possible readership if you are placing ads in newspapers. Lastly, don't forget the value attached to each item. Don't go crazy, but a realistic value helps a sponsor assess the impact of their involvement. This can also be a great way to improve the quality of your advertising. You may find a sponsor who will be interested in upgrading your print to a professional colour brochure in exchange for putting a panel advertising their company on the brochure. A more 'professional look' could then rub off in how others perceive your group.

Meet & Greet.

Do you hold launch events for your shows? Could you have a 'Meet the Cast' function after a show one night for your sponsor and his guests?

The list of benefits are endless. Just have a good think about which items you think might be of most use to your potential sponsor.

THE DEAL

This is the most important part of the proposal. You have discussed your project and what you can give a sponsor, now you need to ask the sponsor for remuneration in return.

Ideally, this should be a short paragraph outlining clearly what you would like the sponsor to provide, whether it be in cash or kind. The bottom line offer is probably one of the most important parts of the proposal.

THE CONCLUSION

Write a brief paragraph telling the sponsor how to reach you and take up your offer if they are interested.

SOME IMPORTANT STUFF

This aforementioned list may sound like basic common sense, but it's amazing how many times groups will supply so much superfluous information that a sponsor won't ever get past the first page. Just remember to keep it simple and honest.

You are approaching a company to take part in a business deal, so act professionally. Present your proposal in a neat, clean and precise way. Keep information in bullet points for easy perusal. Make sure your proposal is accompanied by a covering letter personally addressed to the decision maker you are approaching. If you don't know who that is, find out. Proposals addressed to 'Dear Sir', or 'The Sponsorship Director', often get binned.

In many cases, it would be beneficial to approach local, rather than national sponsors. Think constructively and realistically about who your targets might be.

Think about what you are asking for. Don't just settle for 'support in kind'. You have a lot to offer that can be worth cold, hard, cash.

You don't need to go to the expense of folders and expensive report covers, just keep it simple and effective.

One final thing you need to consider is that some large

companies need planning time to effect a sponsorship relationship. You will have more success if you approach a sponsor months ahead, so forward plan.

Now that you have developed your target list, written your proposal and hopefully been successful in gaining some sponsorship, you may think that you are done, right?

WRONG!

Sponsorship is an ongoing process, that continues before, during and after your show has concluded. Yes, it is a labour intensive process but the benefits can often be staggering. In both Australia and the United States, some groups have their sponsorship process down to such a fine art that it pays for the whole production long before any tickets are sold.

I'm assuming that you have secured some sponsors and are now in the process of staging your event. Here is a very short list of things to consider to help your sponsor get a bigger "bang" for their buck.

Venue Signage - Is there signage in your venue that acknowledges the support of your sponsors? You don't need to go overboard, but some form of acknowledgement is a must.

Sponsor Liaison - Somebody from your group must be on hand front-of-house to meet and greet your sponsor. Do you have a VIP table for collection of tickets? Have you thought about adding in small touches like a free drink voucher? Make sure your sponsor feels like the most important person in the building at all times.

These are just two small things that so many groups get wrong. Once the money is in the bank, they abandon all care of the sponsor, often at their peril. Treat a sponsor right, and more often than not, they'll be open to a repeat performance.

Don't be afraid to keep your sponsor updated as you go along. Make a point of issuing regular updates telling your sponsor how you are going with ticket sales, send copies of media clippings that mention their involvement. Don't be afraid to pitch a story with local media about your sponsor's involvement. This one alone will get you huge brownie points and does a lot for your sponsor's community image.

Once the show is over, gather up a collection of media clippings, reviews, letters from audience members, copies of brochures, some quality production photographs and anything else that quantifies your achievement. Place these items into a presentation album or some form of binder that can be presented to the sponsor as a record of their involvement.

This is a great way for the sponsor to see what their contribution has achieved. Also, they will be able to calculate just how much free publicity they have garnered from an association.

Make sure that your president or chairperson writes a letter of thanks to accompany this package.

Most importantly, ensure that your PR group is fully briefed in what you have agreed with the sponsor, as more often than not, they will be carrying out the deal requirements. Failing to mention the terms could result in their sponsor logo being omitted from an advertisement or press release. A definite disaster in the making.

Sponsorship is not something that companies are obliged to do. For some, it is seen as a community service, for others it is a necessary part of their day-to-day marketing activities. In hard economic times, companies are even more likely to look at sponsorship, as it offers a cost effective way of getting their corporate message out there.

Don't forget that once you have a sponsor on board, it becomes potentially easier to get more. Get your sponsorship team to invite potential sponsors along to your event to see how you treat your existing sponsors and for them to see the exposure that can be gained from an association with your group.

Finally, you can never stop learning about sponsorship methods and techniques. Use other people's success stories to help finesse your plans. There are some great publications out there, but we can recommend the following from personal experience:-

Don't Just Applaud, Send Money!
By Alvin H Reiss.

Angels In American Theatre
By Robert A Shanke et al.

Sponsorship Seekers Toolkit
By Kim Skildum-Reid & Anne-Marie Grey.

Chapter 24 - Thoughts and actions

- Every group, no matter how large or small, is capable of securing a sponsor.

- Be professional in your approach. Sponsors need to take you seriously.

- Research into possible sponsors and what you can offer them is essential as a first step.

- Ensure the deal is in writing, so that both parties have a clear view of what they expect.

25. SURVEYS AND RESEARCH

How will you ever know unless you ask!

Don't ask questions you don't want answers to. You can't please all the people all the time.

So, your shows are poorly attended or your audiences are falling. It's time to start asking some questions.

Whether times are good or bad, it's always a good idea to keep ahead of the curve by asking your audiences for their feedback. Most audiences will give you feedback in abundance if you ask, but it's not for the faint-hearted. Be prepared to be criticised, lampooned, ridiculed and yes, even praised (just a bit).

If you think that members of your company tend to take ownership of your shows, just wait until you see just how much your audience feel they own your company.

Talking to your audience can take many forms and its worth considering some, or all, of these options.

Tell us what you'd like to see.
This is a cynical data capture exercise which I've seen used, and employed myself on many occasions. Small slips are left on every seat asking members of the audience to nominate shows they'd like to see from a set list of, say, 20 possibilities. They are offered a chance to win a gift voucher or VIP theatre experience for taking the trouble if they fill out their name, address, phone number and email address

on the bottom of the form. Forms are then collected after the show in a box in the foyer. Just make sure the table with the box has a few spare pens – not everyone carries one with them!

The cynical part of this exercise is that usually at the bottom of the form, in very small print, is a statement saying that you will be using their information for future contact purposes, unless they tick the box. Most people won't tick the box.

However, you'll also collect a lot of contact information that you can use to market your productions. You also get a list of shows your audience wants to see. Just imagine that you are a contemporary group staging modern musicals that your group love. You do a survey and 95% of your respondents say they want to see *Carousel*, or heaven forbid, even a *Gilbert & Sullivan* operetta! Your group don't want to do it, but your audience want it. What do you do?

I've seen it happen. The group involved staged the musical the audience demanded, only to have a huge sell out and their biggest profit ever. There is no doubt that audience response isn't everything, but it's worth noting the comments. It's all about striking a balance. You might even carefully consider the list of show options presented to the audience for them to choose from.

Online surveys.

There are a number of online survey websites available now that will allow your group to ask questions and poll the results. Try not to make the survey too long. Most people will happily answer 10 – 20 multiple choice questions, but more than that, is pushing it. You can ask questions relating to ticket prices, programme prices, overall experience, theatre comfort, ticket buying experiences, the list is endless. Try to stay focused in your questioning and take note of the comments. Small changes may reap you huge benefits. You may even find the audience thinks you are undercharging for your show – don't laugh with derision, I've seen it happen. Feel free to offer a small incentive. Put respondents into a draw for a prize to say thank you for taking the time to help you.

Discussion Panels.

Have you noticed that one, or a group of your regulars, aren't coming to your shows anymore? Are you getting feedback from certain patrons regularly? Take the time to invite them to a round table feedback forum. Sit down over a coffee or glass of wine and ask them for their opinions. Show you care what they think and that you want to improve the service offered. When people are treated well and made to feel special, they tend to try to help with constructive criticism. You don't have to agree with all of it, but I know I'd rather hear comments directly than have someone complaining behind my back. Some small gems often result from this process and it's amazing how that panel will feel more comfortable talking to you in future. Just don't be defensive – listen objectively and have open discussions.

Website feedback.

Make sure your website encourages people to send you feedback. Patrons appreciate an opportunity to easily make a comment, be it good or bad. Make sure that they can do so easily. Most importantly, ensure someone receives the comment, notes it and sends a simple thank you note so the person who submits it knows they've been heard.

Use the feedback you collect when making your PR and management decisions. What is the point of collecting valuable feedback if you relegate it to the rubbish bin without debate and consideration?

Chapter 25 - Thoughts and actions

• Feedback from an audience is an important marketing tool.

• Utilise various mediums to get your audience talking to you.

• Thank contributors for their feedback.

26. PRESS NIGHT

It all comes down to tonight.

Don't think that all your hard work is over once you get to opening night. Possibly some of the most important moments in your PR campaign lie ahead of you.

It's Press Night!

Who to invite?
Press night can invariably see your team beset by a group of people seeking nothing more than 'freebies' to your show. The trick is to refine the list, seek out those who you feel should be attending and ensuring you get as much coverage as possible. A good mix of press, local celebrities or dignitaries, sponsors and potential benefactors is essential. Don't forget that you need a liberal mix of friends too to ensure a good audience reaction.

Whilst any press comment is good, make sure you have a good mix of reviewers who will give you considered and weighty reviews that can be used for your long-term PR overview. Ensure that you also have media that can get your review out immediately. Reviews during your run will help convince any last minute stragglers that they need to buy a ticket.

The Night Itself.
It's always important to have your PR team in full swing on press night.

Set up a Press / VIP desk in the foyer to allow press and dignitaries to bypass box office queues.

Try to ensure that you have given your press guests good quality seats. Don't put all the press together if you can help it, space them out across the auditorium, so they get a feel for the real audience wherever possible.

I suggest that each member of the press should be afforded their two tickets, a complimentary programme and ideally, vouchers for a drink at interval.

Make a point of introducing yourself, thank them for coming. If reviewing for a website or publication, let them know that you will be sending them images.

This is your moment to build on your existing relationship and show the press that you are professional and thoughtful.

Whatever you do though, don't overcrowd them. Welcome them, be helpful if necessary, then allow them to enjoy the show experience for themselves. Always be on hand after the show at the press desk just in case.

The next day as a courtesy, send an email or place a call thanking them for coming and asking if they need anything further from you. Be on hand for any clarifications or further photo requests they have.

HOW TO USE REVIEWS

No matter whether you are a West End Producer or a small town theatre group PR team, many of us have used the review edit to our benefit.

I've seen a West End review that read "*This could have been a good show*" cut to "*A good show*". You see the power of the edit.

No mater how tempting it is, you must never change the context of the comment in your edit. Reviewers will have your guts for garters if you mess with their intentions, and believe me there's nothing worse that a reviewer whose irked, not to mention what Trading Standards would say!

As the recipient of the review, you are permitted to quote sections of the review in your PR material, in advertisements, in emails, or on your website. In fact, anywhere that you see fit.

Make sure any quote you run includes the name of the media outlet where it was published. Even the names of the reviewers themselves are starting to appear in some PR material.

Placing quotes on your website can help assure potential new audiences over time that your shows are of quality and worth seeing.

In exactly the same way that you rely on reviews before shelling out for a trip, movie ticket, book or CD, many patrons will look to see what the critics think of your show before purchasing a ticket.

Front of House display.
Whether you are staging a play or musical, consider a front of house display board featuring production photos, reviews and cast photographs. Not only do they provide an item of interest during performances, but passers-by

during the day might be prompted to buy a ticket if the display is interesting.

Chapter 26 - Thoughts and actions

• Tickets are valuable. Plan your invitation list carefully.

• Try to get reviews out before the show closes if at all possible.

• Have a Front Of House Press Contact Point in place.

• Personal contact with the media on press night is important.

• Follow up after press night.

• Use review quotes honestly and carefully with proper accreditation to the author and media source.

27. NOT ALL PR IS GOOD PR

Choose carefully and don't be afraid to say no.

There are some PR officers who are more than happy to snap up any offers of publicity that fall their way, but I'd like to suggest that this may not always be the best way to operate.

Most offers of publicity are generally great opportunities to promote your group and your show, but take the time to examine each offer as it comes in and look at the short and long term impact of how that publicity might affect you.

In the past few years, many companies have been lured by the offers of TV companies hoping that their few minutes of exposure on the television might just change their fortunes.

For the most part, these TV appearances are on local news programmes or relate to larger festivals or events, which really do benefit your group.

Some companies have fallen foul though of the offer of reality TV, only to wish afterwards that they had kept away.

Don't forget that the power of television lies in the person with editorial control. Taking part in any documentary or 'fly on the wall' series may initially seem like a good offer, but don't forget TV relies on conflict, laughs and drama to keep audiences entertained. Many amateur theatre groups are seen by the outside world as hapless groups of 'wannabe stars' with little or no talent. Whilst we know that is not the case, you can see how it might make for better television to make even the most professional theatre group look like their productions are blunder-ridden and doomed to fail to keep audiences tuned in.

Likewise, some groups have fallen foul of the tabloid press of late on a variety of sensitive issues such as race. Each situation needs to be judged on its relative merits, but never be afraid to issue a simple "no comment" to the press. Sometimes trying to put your side of an argument forward can prove futile and simply serve to prolong the media battle. Someone once said that today's news is tomorrow's fish and chip wrappings. Whilst that is no longer the case due to the power of the internet, sometimes saying nothing is the best response.

Take the time to think about the long-term effect that any PR offer might have on your company. Take care to project a professional image that reflects the way you want your company to be viewed by the world. Your reputation or brand is one of your most valuable assets and must never be undervalued. Whilst it may mean passing up on some opportunities in the short-term, in the long-term you will build credibility and a reputation for professionalism that will be the envy of your peers.

Chapter 27 - Thoughts and actions

- Take a brief moment to think about media requests. Do they fit what you want from the media?

- Don't just say 'yes' to everything. If it doesn't feel right, it might not be for you.

- Media reports hang around in the current climate. Be careful what is said by you and about you. It may come back to haunt you.

28. CASE STUDY: DARLINGTON OPERATIC SOCIETY

I spoke to Julian Cound from Darlington Operatic Society about their efforts when it comes to PR, having been impressed by some of the media campaigns they have undertaken in recent years:

"DarlingtonOS has a history dating back over 70 years of presenting high quality musicals at the beautiful 900-seater Civic Theatre. When looking at marketing initiatives for the two musicals we present each year, like every other amateur theatre group, we have a very difficult job to do. We put on 2 full-scale shows a year, each running for 10 nights (11 performances if we hold a matinee).

"Things would be a lot easier if we were selling, say, a bar of chocolate. We would research what people liked, mass produce it, sell it. It becomes successful so we continue making the same bar of chocolate year in, year out, and it keeps selling. However, what we are producing is a completely different bar of chocolate every six months. We have to work out who will like each bar of chocolate (as not everyone will like every different bar we make) then we have to find how best to market each bar of chocolate to ensure the right people know we have made something they will apreciate. Knowing what people will like (or dislike) is the hardest job of all.

"All of you reading this have a similar interest in amateur theatre, but I can guarantee there will be shows that some of you like or dislike, shows that you would buy a ticket for and those you would not.

"We need to ensure we are an attractive proposition in terms of value for money, production values, ease of purchase, customer service and it is imperative for us all to improve our brand awareness. The term brand awareness may sound rather 'professional' but, like it or not, we are in the professional market. People buying a ticket to your production (whether they be in a village hall or a 2000-seater theatre) are buying into your brand. You have to ensure your brand has value, is protected from any potential negative press and is constantly policed to ensure it is still something people want to buy into.

"Like it or not, we are all in competition with the likes of Showcase Cinemas, Gala Casinos, Gyms, Restaurants and Sky TV. Unless we start using similar marketing practices and match the levels of customer service these companies use day in, day out, we will always come off worse.

"For many, a trip to the theatre is now a luxury – we have to ensure that someone's trip to see our shows is the best theatre experience they receive – from the moment they book their ticket to the moment they leave the theatre after the performance.

"Over the last few years, we have started getting involved in more and more local events to put ourselves in front of new audiences who may not see us in the theatre. If people see our product in surroundings they are familiar with first, they may be inclined to visit us in the theatre.

"Interestingly, a lot of these initiatives can be done for little or no money. As Marketing Manager for DarlingtonOS,

I am often asked how we can spend so much money on promoting our shows. In reality, the actual spend is quite low. Word of mouth, social media, press coverage, radio coverage (not advertising) is all absolutely free of charge and it is here where you have to be creative.

"Gone are the days when sticking up a poster in the local chip shop will ensure a full house. You have to look at your usual methods of marketing and ask yourself "is this really as effective as it could be?". Take a lead from other societies and other brands. If you see a campaign you think is quite clever, ask yourself how that could be moulded to fit your next show – there are no new ideas out there, just the same ideas made to fit a new situation.

"Tracking any marketing campaign is essential to ensure you know how effective it has been. Unfortunately, for most amateur theatre companies, tracking marketing is not always possible due to time, money or knowledge. For our current production (*Footloose*) we have set up online purchasing through TicketSource – this system allows you to ask several questions of every person who books through the system. One question we ask is how they heard about the show? It is clear from the answers given so far that every marketing campaign we have run has produced ticket sales – some more than others. This information will allow us to determine which to pursue for future productions.

"Working with TicketSource has already brought in over 200 *new* names to DarlingtonOS – these are not necessarily new customers, but they are people we had no contact details for, now they are added to our database. 200 full contact details (name, address, email, mobile) of your core marketing audience is priceles. And this number is steadily growing day by day.

"Information and communication is everything. If you don't know what is (or is not) happening there is nothing you can do to affect it. We now have up-to-the-minute ticket sales information broken down to specific areas of the theatre on each night. If one night is not selling as well as it should, we can put a simple incentive out to encourage people to book on that night, we can send a quick email round to our membership to encourage friends to book on that night – anything to bring the nightly average sales up to the level we need to reach break-even as quickly as possible. The instantaneous nature of the internet is invaluable for this.

"Without the detailed information required, all our shows are marketed using a blanket method. In real terms, it takes someone to see a sales message over eight times before they are influenced to do anything about it. We spread our marketing wide – newspaper editorial, posters, radio, theatre brochure, pro-tour programmes, Facebook, Twitter, website, Amateur Stage magazine. In this way we can be sure we have done our best to get as much exposure as possible.

"You may feel that people will get sick of hearing your message. But you must believe in your product, believe in your brand, be positive and encourage everyone involved in your brand to be positive. Then, and only then, will you start to see a difference."

Recently Darlington undertook two bold promotion plans, both of which paid off in different and unexpected ways. In 2012, Darlington posted this photo on Facebook to promote their October production of Footloose. The picture lead many people to comment about how not all groups could afford such lavish marketing, and started a viral conversation, that was seen by almost a thousand people. One small thing though, the picture was a mock up, no such public location with a *Footloose* poster existed. Darlington's little Photoshop gimmick had ensured that people took notice of their forthcoming production and started talking about it. As a piece of free publicity, its results were remarkable.

During the preparation for their recent production of Maury Yeston's *Titanic*, Peter Barron, Editor of the Northern Echo newspaper, became involved in their production of *Titanic* following a hopeful email to him to see if he would be interested in a 'walk-on' part in one performance as W T Stead the former Editor of the Northern Echo (based in Darlington) who died on the original Titanic. This was to be a simple promotional ploy to get a few extra column centimetres in the newspaper. In fact, it snowballed. Peter fell in love with the society, saw the huge benefits they bring to the Civic Theatre and Darlington, the passion and dedication. So much so, that Peter is now the first Honorary Patron, who works tirelessly to help promote amateur theatre in general.

Darlington are constantly using a combination of edgy and classic promotion techniques to market their shows with great dividends. Their success shows that a little initiative and a lot of professionalism go a long way.

Find out more information at
www.darlingtonoperaticsociety.org.uk

29. CASE STUDY. SEDOS - LONDON

About Sedos.

With a membership of over 200, a programme of around eight to ten challenging fringe theatre productions every year and a reputation for West End quality in every production, Sedos are proud of their claim to be the premier amateur theatre group in London.

The acting and producing membership includes an eclectic mix from all over London, but maintains strong links with the City via its members from investment banks, law firms, brokers, the Exchanges and many other financial and city-based firms. Sedos are an unincorporated association run by an executive committee and a registered charity (no. 1099443). They maintain a strong emphasis not only on member participation but also on excellence, as the reputation of the society grows within the community.

The society was founded in 1905 by a group of senior members of the Stock Exchange, led by Charles Dickinson and Cyril Bathurst, who formed the Dramatic and Operatic Society. Their principal aims were twofold:

To take advantage of the great variety of stage talent they saw scattered around the house, and;

To use what was no doubt an actual extension of the virtuoso talent employed by the members on the trading floor at the time to raise funds for charity.

Stephen Beeny took time out to talk to me about how Sedos operate.

Q: Sedos has a marketing sub committee. How many people sit on that committee? Are they autonomous from the main committee? How do they inter-relate to each other?

There are currently four key members of the Sedos marketing subcommittee and about four or five others who also contribute. Because we are not an elected committee, the number is quite fluid and we are very happy to accept anyone who offers their help. We meet about six times a year. We work independently from the main elected Sedos committee on marketing shows and also more general marketing of the society, but we are in constant discussion with the main committee. Among our number, we always have a committee liaison person, who sits on both the main committee and the marketing subcommittee and acts as a constant "go between" making sure information goes both ways. Among the four key marketing subcommittee members, we each have a particular ongoing responsibility - one person for the website and social media (Stephen Beeny), one for our weekly newsletter (Chris Warner), one for press (Adrian Johnson), one for our quarterly e-magazine and liaison with other companies (Pippa Roome). We are also in the process of adding a person with responsibility for schools and universities. For each show, there is a "marketing lead" - sometimes this is someone from the marketing subcommittee, but other times it is another member who the individual show team recruit and we then support. We have also put together a Comms Guide, which is a written "how to" on marketing a Sedos show. But we are all very much still learning and we don't pretend to have all the answers!

Q. How many shows does Sedos stage each year, with how

many performances?

We stage around eight to ten main shows a year, plus often a workshop production or two. Included are normally two 'two-week' musicals (11 performances), while other shows (a mix of plays and musicals) are normally one week (six performances). We are currently the resident theatre company at the Bridewell Theatre and have 10 weeks a year there, plus we also perform in other venues. In total, in 2012 we will do 68 full performances, plus a workshop performance of *6plays, 7days* – a project where members wrote, directed, rehearsed and staged six 10-minute new plays in just seven days.

Q. You sell a lot of tickets online. What sort of feedback do you get from clients about not having phone or postal bookings? Any pros and cons about the system?

We only have an online box office, we don't have any official system for phone or postal bookings. In general, this works well. We do get occasional calls from people who don't have internet access, or have a query - we don't have a "Sedos phone number" but we try to give the Bridewell Theatre a number for the producer/marketing lead for each show in case they get calls and some producers/marketing leads will also put their personal number on listings sites. When we get these calls, we can feed the booking through the site by simply taking the person's details over the phone and booking them in. But we would expect to take less than 20 calls per show and most of these are queries rather than bookings. The big advantage of the system is that no one has to be responsible for manning a phone or taking bookings; the disadvantage is that we probably lose a small number of sales to those who cannot book online.

Q. Sedos has been very pro-active with their online marketing campaigns. Is social media a major factor in all your campaigns and is it effective?

Yes, it's a major factor. Ongoing Facebook content is always something we look at particularly when we plan a show's marketing and we believe it helps sell tickets in terms of reminding the members and Facebook fans to book, and hopefully spreading the Sedos word to the friends of the show team. We try and publish one post each week day about the shows, but also Sedos itself. To us, developing the Sedos band is equally as important as selling tickets. So far, we've been slightly less pro-active on twitter – lacking time and resource in terms of someone to keep the account active – but we are improving this too.

Q. How important is tracking of sales data when you plan your PR campaigns?

For each show, our treasurer (Craig Topp) gives us a weekly update on ticket sales from six weeks prior to opening night, with comparisons to other shows which were similar in terms of run length and projected sales. This is really useful because most of our shows sell quite late which can be nerve-racking, so having comparisons gives marketing leads and producers an idea of how they are doing and whether they need to panic or not!

Q. You work hard to encourage your casts to help sell tickets. Can you tell me some of the more interesting methods you use to get the cast involved?

We believe 90% of our ticket sales come from friends and family of the cast and crew, so we make sure that the team have everything they need to sell the show to their connections - hard copy flyers and email versions and things like photos which they can use as cover and profile pictures on Facebook. We also make sure every show has a Facebook event and encourage the cast and crew to invite friends to it. We try to build an ongoing "story" on social media - photos, videos, fun little items on Facebook, etc - which people can like, tag and comment on, to make the show more visible on social media to friends of the cast and crew. Another tactic we have used is a weekly sales update, so we pass on the top line figures from the treasurer to the team each week, so they know if we are on track. We've also had some success with a "bonus budget" tactic - we get the treasurer's agreement to spend slightly more money if we can clock good sales figures at an early stage, and we use that to get cast to buy into the process, telling them if we sell more tickets they will get better costumes, set, etc. Apart from that, it's just good old-fashioned nagging!

Q. Is there anything you do PR wise that really works for Sedos above anything else?

Not sure! The difficult thing about marketing is that it's hard to know what has worked when it goes well or what hasn't when it doesn't. We have recently included a question on our box office asking buyers where they heard about us, so we are in the early stages of analysing that data. One thing I think we have improved since the marketing subcommittee came in (start of 2010), is starting our marketing early, getting box offices open a bit earlier, having flyers at the previous show, getting adverts for upcoming shows in programmes and so on. We have also tried to improve on selling the Sedos brand - better consistency in terms of brand guidelines for print publicity, improved website, including review quotes on our website, having a "season postcard" which people can pick up at shows or in the Bridewell, which lists the whole season and has information about the company.

Q. You stage a lot of themed nights for charity – aside from helping good causes does it have any residual benefit for Sedos above public goodwill?

It offers us some marketing opportunities - for example our current charity of the year is *Mousetrap Theatre Projects* and we are able to offer discounted tickets to their young people mailing lists. I think the charity angle also helps when we approach people for sponsorship and to ask for free things! We also have quite a lot of themed nights which are not for charity - the "standard" is a gala night with a higher ticket price and a glass of fizz and a programme included, but we've also done others which perhaps tie into a theme or setting of the show and they have been successful, giving us a "novelty value" to sell. For example, the middle Saturday matinee of a musical is traditionally the hardest to sell, but it was the first performance of *A Little Night Music* (2011) to sell out when we marketed it as a Fika Matinee Tea, with a free cup of tea/coffee and brownie (sponsored by Swedish restaurant Fika) pre-show.

Q. You've staged some quite interesting shows that many mainstream groups wouldn't touch. Is there a show or style of show that Sedos just couldn't make work?

From a marketing point of view, hopefully not! Some shows are more difficult to sell than others and we try to set our sales aims accordingly - so for example, we might budget to sell 500-600 tickets on a popular play with a decent cast size, but only 350 for a lesser known show with a small cast. As well as show type, we find time of year and the position in the season compared to other shows makes a difference. For example, our Summer Festival this year was quite a tough job from a sales point of view because our focus was split across three shows (including one double bill, so actually, four shows!) and three special events. Sedos tries to produce darker, less well-known shows. This has given us a reputation for innovation and quality that keeps audiences and actors coming back for more.

Q. How important is the customer experience when they come to a Sedos show?

Very - I like to think that if audience members have a positive experience, from friendly front of house and box office staff, to a professional-standard show, they will both come back and recommend us to their friends. It's also worth noting that to us the audience experience begins before they come and see the show. Our website is our shop window on to the world, and we are proud to keep this updated and full of interesting content, so that new audiences and potential members can find out more about us, view our past production details and photos and book tickets.

Sedos look well placed as they head towards the future. 2011 was the first year in which every main Sedos show (excluding workshop productions) has made a profit - that's obviously about budget/spend control as well as marketing. The group impresses me with their open thinking, progressive marketing and ability to offer information, relevant stories and articles to the press to help with their ticket sales.

Find out more information at
www.sedos.co.uk

30. ARE YOU READY?

Over the preceding chapters, we have looked at all aspects of the publicity process and I trust that you have found it helpful.

It's time now for you to go out and implement your PR plan. Before you start though, a few final points:-

1. Allow enough time – the publicity process begins before auditions do. Don't leave your PR efforts until the last minute or it will be your undoing. Plan everything in advance and leave plenty of time.

2. Ask for help – If you need assistance ask. Never battle on under duress. People will be willing to help you if you ask. The best bit about having a PR team (even if it's only two of you) is that you can support each other.

3. Enjoy your triumphs – You know what they say about 'all work and no play'? PR is never an easy job, but when it goes right, take a bit of time to pat yourself on the back – you deserve it. Make a point of telling people like Amateur Stage or other media outlets about your triumphs. We like to publish good news and show other people how it's done when groups have success.

I'm looking forward to seeing your campaigns and to hearing about how things have gone for your group as you move forward.

Finally, if you've tried something we haven't covered, and

it worked, please let me know. We'd love to include new methods in the 2nd Edition of Packed To The Rafters to keep our offering to you as current as it can be.

Enjoy and may all your houses be full!

Douglas Mayo
October 2012.

USEFUL RESOURCES

Amateur Stage Magazine
www.amateurstagemagazine.co.uk

Amdram.co.uk
www.amdram.co.uk

Words & Music
www.words-and-music.info

Sardines Magazine
www.sardinesmagazine.co.uk

MAILING LIST SOFTWARE PROVIDERS

Your Mailing List
www.yourmailinglistprovider.com

Constant Contact
www.constantcontact.com

Mail Chimp
www.mailchimp.com

Mailing Manager
www.mailingmanager.co.uk

Dot Mailer
www.dotmailer.co.uk

E-Shot
www.e-shot.net

WEBSITE SERVICES

Moonfruit
www.moonfruit.com

Wix
www.wix.com

1 and 1
www.1and1.co.uk

Webs
www.webs.com

Weebly
www.weebly.com

Spanglefish
www.spanglefish.com

ONLINE TICKETING PROVIDERS

Ticket Source
www.ticketsource.co.uk

Positickets
www.positickets.co.uk

NODA Box Office
www.nodaboxoffice.co.uk

Little Box Office
www.littleboxoffice.com

Made in the USA
Lexington, KY
08 January 2013